DEMAND HORIZON

DEMAND HORIZON

A Revolutionary Approach to Creating Great Products

GERRY CAMPBELL

Advantage®

Published by Advantage, Charleston, South Carolina.
Member of Advantage Media Group.

ADVANTAGE is a registered trademark and the Advantage colophon is a trademark of Advantage Media Group, Inc.

Printed in the United States of America.

ISBN: 978-159932-412-8
LCCN: 2013952355

This publication is designed to provide accurate and authoritative information in regard to the subject matter covered. It is sold with the understanding that the publisher is not engaged in rendering legal, accounting, or other professional services. If legal advice or other expert assistance is required, the services of a competent professional person should be sought.

Advantage Media Group is proud to be a part of the Tree Neutral® program. Tree Neutral offsets the number of trees consumed in the production and printing of this book by taking proactive steps such as planting trees in direct proportion to the number of trees used to print books. To learn more about Tree Neutral, please visit **www.treeneutral.com**. To learn more about Advantage's commitment to being a responsible steward of the environment, please visit **www.advantagefamily.com/green**

Advantage Media Group is a publisher of business, self-improvement, and professional development books and online learning. We help entrepreneurs, business leaders, and professionals share their Stories, Passion, and Knowledge to help others Learn & Grow. Do you have a manuscript or book idea that you would like us to consider for publishing? Please visit **advantagefamily.com** or call **1.866.775.1696**.

My goal is to empower product creators in companies of all sizes to think more precisely about how market demand shapes the products that they create and help them to attain a new degree of certainty in the process.

ACKNOWLEDGEMENTS

Frequency Group; Travis Corrigan, Adam Kaslikow-
ski and Greg Snow, whose priceless contributions in
the form of ideas, conversations and sweat are represented in these pages. And to the honorary team Mike
Blackwell, Ben Hadley and Dr. Robert Wuebker, your
influence has been monumental.

Brian Solis who was kind enough to provide his
thoughts in the foreword, as well as his advice and perspective on both Demand Horizon and my previous
company.

My mentors Ho Blair, Vance Caesar and Jeff Hudson,
who each helped me refine my thinking and jam-pack
my love of technology products into 22,000 words.

My extensive network of friends and colleagues who
served as sounding boards, reality-checks and masters

of gentle redirection—particularly Arthur Brodeur, David Schrieberg, Sam Uretsky and Krista Thomas. I won't be filling your inboxes with drafts for a while, I know you'll miss that.

The people I've had the opportunity to work with in product creation, business partner relationships, investments and advisory capacities.

The team at Advantage Media Group who guided me through the process of this first book. More books to follow.

C O N T E N T S

Innovate or Die!

The demand horizon process gets at the heart of the changes that are transforming business today. Customers are in control, now and forever into the future. The model presented in this book provides a roadmap for building products and creating businesses that are aligned with the new rules of marketing.

In 1999 Rick Levine, Christopher Locke, Doc Searls and David Weinberger published the *The Cluetrain Manifesto*. The book represented a set of 95 theses that translated into a call to action for businesses of all shapes and sizes to change with the rise of the Internet. The authors' hypothesized that the Internet ushered in a social economy that would bring about the end of business as usual.[1]

> *Through the Internet, people are discovering and inventing new ways to share relevant knowledge with blinding speed. As a direct result, markets are getting smarter—and getting smarter faster than most companies. Today's markets are conversations. Their members communicate in language that is natural, open, honest, direct, funny, and often shocking. Companies that aren't listening to these exchanges are missing a dire warning. Companies that aren't engaging in them are missing an unprecedented opportunity.*

— THE CLUETRAIN MANIFESTO

Now at over a decade old, their message rings louder and truer today. With the pervasiveness of today's social and mobile media, customers are not only more connected, they're more informed. As a result, your customers are empowered and they're increasingly discerning, demanding, and impatient. These connected customers expect companies to listen. They want to be

---

1 http://books.google.com/books/about/The_Cluetrain_Manifesto.html

engaged. And experiences prevail above products and services.

This isn't just the end of business as usual; this is an era when consumers insist on taking business personally.

Forcing customers through outdated sales funnels isn't going to improve relationships or experiences. Unleashing the wrath of aging service models and leaving customers to fend for themselves through diabolical call center jungles is, in hindsight, ridiculous.

Instead, we will explore new horizons to build the foundations of tomorrow—today.

To compete today, right now, in both real time and at the right time, takes competing for the future. The way people make decisions, how we support them, how we meet expectations, how we design products and services that meet unmet needs, how we reduce friction, is made easier by embracing innovation, objectivity and always considering possibilities and opportunities.

As always, actions speak louder than words. New frameworks are needed. New processes are needed. But more importantly, a new vision and overarching philosophy is essential to lead us away from a culture of management and mediocrity to a culture of leadership and innovation. For, if we're not competing for the future, we are only competing for the moment—and thus irrelevance.

Innovation begins with the desire to do something that is meaningful. And all effort starts with a drive to understand the needs of the customer. A business that is rooted in the customer and enlivened by vision, passion and resilience can participate in this time of unprecedented opportunity. Let's get to work.

#innovateordie

— B R I A N   S O L I S , Principal, Altimeter Group and author of the bestselling books *The End of Business as Usual, Engage!* and *What's the Future of Business (WTF)*

A Tale of Lost Opportunity

"This world is clearly emerging before our eyes. The shifts ahead, the opportunities ahead are massive."

— CARLY FIORINA, regarding HP's
acquisition of Compaq in 2002

I remember it as if it were yesterday. I stepped onto the elevator of Compaq HQ in Houston and there stood a guy with a crazy contraption in his hand. I had never seen anything like it before. It looked as if someone had taken a hard drive, strapped a camcorder battery to it, and jammed some headphones into an exposed jack on a raw circuit board. I had to ask, "What is that thing?"

"It's an mp3 player," he said. Then he explained to me that he had hundreds of digitized songs on the hard drive. My mind struggled to comprehend. This was in June 1998. At that point in time there were no mp3 players on the market. Apple wouldn't launch the iPod until 2001, and the Diamond Rio player wouldn't be announced for another few months. And yet there I was on the elevator at Compaq HQ with a guy who had an mp3 player in his hand. It was amazing.

In retrospect, what strikes me about that encounter was that Compaq had a prototype for a device that would ultimately change the world. The company had every capability to take it to market. Instead, it missed the opportunity to define, or even participate, in the emerging market. To understand this situation and propose an alternate path that could have led to success is to understand the core of demand-driven product creation. Compaq started as a portable-computer company. The very first Compaq computer was mobile—not by today's standards but certainly by the standards of the day. In addition to mobile computing, the company had an R&D lab that had developed technology enabling e-commerce, mobile computing, and digital entertainment.

Yet, when HP eventually bought out Compaq in September 2001, the company was profoundly weak at cultivating new markets. Compaq had not found a way to remain relevant, despite all of the experimental technologies in their labs. It's such a stunning contrast, considering that there were absolutely transformational technologies owned, developed, and managed from within, and yet they could not save their own life. It's not good enough to innovate, and this is an all-too-common tale. Product creators must understand the unmet needs of the customer and explore beyond the known horizon of the market to sense where opportunities lie. Technology itself—or any value proposition for that matter—is useless until customers express a need for it and that need is discovered.

That's the core idea behind the demand horizon model: it's a mental model, or framework, for understanding market-driven demand. Understanding demand is the single most critical thing a company can do to ensure its success. Compaq's story is so poignant because it had all of the pieces before the game even started in mobile computing, but the company lost because it couldn't sense customer demand as well as its competitors.

Had Compaq understood the potential demand for digital music, there would've been clear focus on moving those products through to development and ultimately out to the market. Compaq's fate could have been very different had it focused on an innovation model that allowed it to understand user demand.

Had Compaq done some exploration to discover that a huge appetite for digital music existed, it would've been obvious that it should take that crazy contraption from the elevator and put a lot of horsepower behind it. Who knows, had Compaq done so, maybe people would be lining up outside Compaq stores, waiting for the release of Compaq's latest iPaq smartphone.

The Origin of Demand Horizon

In the past 10 years there have been substantial advances in the craft of new business creation. We have witnessed the rise in popularity of entrepreneurship, the advancement of scientific techniques for discovering business opportunities and the proliferation of accelerator environments for fostering creativity and speed the process of success. And that is just for start-ups. On the corporate side we have seen near-universal adoption of agile development variants, an explosion of intrapreneurship programs and rapid product development techniques deployed to great result.

As a lifetime entrepreneur and intrapreneur, I have had the opportunity to witness and participate in the most exciting time in human history. My grandchildren will be regaled by stories of how I met Steve Jobs, Elon Musk and the Google guys. I also know we, as an industry, have a long way to go to learn how to create great products with confidence.

Failure rates are too high. Too much money is spent on products that fail too quickly. Too many important days are wasted on ideas that will never find a market. And too few passionate entrepreneurs are making their desired impact. This is where my experience and perspective can be of some use.

This book is for all those who want to improve their world and the lives of others through the creation of great products. It's for technologist inventors who want their brilliance and precision to reach the most users. It's for businesspeople who want to build profitable businesses that serve the needs of their customers. It's for product managers who can envision new ways to meet emerging needs. It's for user-experience people who believe design and creativity should have a broad impact on the products we use. Throughout the book all of these various audiences are collectively called product creators.

Additionally, these concepts deal largely with consumer markets and technology products. It is my hope that the examples, illustrations and concepts are simple, clear and impactful. The principle of customer demand lies at the core of all successful businesses but these ideas may require adaptation for other markets such as business-to-business, enterprise, packaged goods and professional services.

Throughout the book are principles that have been captured in many different ways by many different approaches. There are generous helpings of ideas that are similar to those in design thinking, agile methodology, the lean start-up philosophy, and so on. Rather than retrace that history, I aim to place this book on the shoulders of those giants, taking the principles that apply to this approach and leaving out what doesn't. The primary contribution of this book is that it reorients product creation around a new understanding of user demand. It doesn't just take users into account for validation of ideas; it centers the entire product creation process on the discovery and interpretation of demand. That, I believe, is a meaningful contribution to the previously mentioned approaches.

Many of the case studies, examples and illustrations are of companies, products and approaches that failed to understand fully the new balance of the demand economy. These stories, when coupled with explanations of how the same situation could have been addressed differently, become powerful contrasts. They illustrate how different the two approaches are and what is now required of companies to be successful. No criticism is intended, the examples are for understanding and clarity, chosen because these are situations that can be understood by the largest possible audience.

Who *isn't* this book for? The insights in the book are derived from experience, interpretation and collaboration with other tech pioneers. As such it has immediate application to today's challenges but doesn't follow the style or exhaustive detail of an academic work. So for those who would seek the academic standard of peer-reviewed validation, you will have to wait. There is still a significant amount to be understood about the topic of demand-driven product creation. Exploration of the topic will proceed deeper in the future.

And this book is certainly a starting point. It was hard to decide where this book should end and the next should begin. As you will see, we have had a fundamental reversal of the supply/demand equation, a balance that has been in place for the entirety of our modern day. The implications are significant and the opportunity, if understood, is unparalleled.

CHAPTER ONE

Bringing Certainty to Innovation

"The image of the world around us, which we carry in our head, is just a model. Nobody in his head imagines all the world, government or country. He has only selected concepts, and relationships between them, and uses those to represent the real system."

— JAY WRIGHT FORRESTER

Creating new products is hard. It's even harder to make things the market really wants. Every product manager, technology exec and start-up entrepreneur knows this. Why is it so hard? There are several reasons: making things that haven't existed before can be technically challenging; it can be difficult to get a team, with all of the various pieces of the creation, onto the same page about what's being built.

However, those problems are small in comparison to the real issue: to create something new that users want, product creators have to discern what the market cannot express. The problem is that people cannot tell you what they want if they haven't seen it before.[2]

As product creators, we deal with this in several ways. Often we craft a motivating vision, something that the team and the market can grasp and rally around. Sometimes we trust our sense of trends and predict what features and uses the customers will find valuable. In some cases we even drive product creation out of sheer passion and commitment. Many times all of the above are backed by market research, industry analysis and vast experience. But that's not enough.

The truth is until now it has all been guesswork. Success is spotty, at best. There is a far better way to discover user need and create products and resulting businesses that have natural fit. It is possible to have significantly more confidence in the products your company develops,

---

2 Samuelson, P. A., 1948, "Consumption Theory in Terms of Revealed Preference," *Economica*, New Series 15, no. 60: 243–253

regardless of the company's stage. To take advantage of this new approach, we have to leave some old ideas behind. First of all, the goal is to forego ego, vision and determination—or at least delay it—in exchange for an objective process that discovers and seeks to understand what users can't express verbally. The objective is to find existing demand in the market just like a natural resource. It cannot be willed into being. It can only be isolated, understood and cultivated. This is a process of discovery, not of drive. When the need is found, passion has a place. Second, there needs to be a new fundamental understanding about how markets work. Our business environment has reversed polarity in terms of the supply/demand balance.[3]

Everything is different. The product creator must let go of traditional understanding about how to define products and reorient the product creation process around the new driver of customer demand. Third, this new orientation to market demand redefines how we think about companies and the progression through the market over time. With this new mental model we can address product creation at each stage of life with accuracy and effectiveness.

---

3 Kash, R., 2002, *The New Law of Demand and Supply: The Revolutionary New Demand Strategy for Faster Growth and Higher Profits,* New York: Doubleday Business, 2002

Some people are naturally talented innovators, understanding what consumers want when they cannot articulate it. That had always been Steve Jobs' special type of magic. However, not everyone is born with that innate talent. The good news is that innovation doesn't need to be the domain of a gifted few. Understanding innovation and how to discover new markets is a process of breaking user demand down into its component pieces.[4] Doing so allows a more precise understanding of how things work and how to manage and optimize the various pieces of the system. By drilling deep and breaking down customer demand into its component pieces, it can be approached with a logical, repeatable method that can be adjusted and improved over time. Innovation activities can be managed, repeated, optimized and ultimately de-risked like any other business activity. You just need to know how to approach it. By understanding this process it is possible to achieve insight into what potential customers want, even before they know what they want themselves.

There's nothing mystical here. The demand horizon approach starts with the notion of market demand and

---

4 Ahuja, G., and R. Katila, 2002, "Something Old, Something New: A Longitudinal Study of Search Behavior and New Product Introduction," *Academy of Management Journal* 45, no. 6: 1183–1194

breaks it down into component parts for study and optimization.

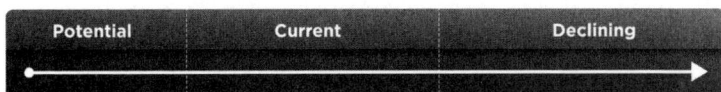

Potential	Current	Declining

The demand horizon model is based on the idea that not all innovation is the same. As the diagram above shows, that continuum starts at the left with "Potential" (demand). Within potential demand, there is a need within a growing number of potential customers. When there is a solution for that burgeoning need, a market can form. From there a market is formed around the "Current" (demand) and the need is actively satisfied. That's the stage where market players know what they want and how to compete to get there. From there follows "Declining" (demand), which is self-explanatory. The underlying idea is that consumer demand constantly changes and new markets are materializing from the vague realm of potential demand. The innovative products we create are solutions to needs that are often beyond the visible horizon. Managing the demand horizon effectively provides the ability to understand where emerging product opportunities lie. When you know that, you have a much better chance to compete and establish leadership. Without that knowledge, it becomes very difficult to build and sustain businesses. The aim is to understand how ideas move through the demand horizon—from what was previously a very vaguely expressed need to something that becomes a real opportunity for business.

CHAPTER TWO

The Big Shift

"There is a supply for every demand."

— FLORENCE SCOVEL SHINN

I n case you haven't noticed it, the world has changed. By that, I don't just mean that the latest iPhone is faster and the new Android phone has a screen as big as your head. I mean *big* change. In the last 10 years we've seen a fundamental flip-flop in the way successful businesses create and market products. Simply put, we've gone from a world where companies create products and push them to users via sales and marketing to users to a world where the users themselves have taken over, pulling to themselves only the products they desire.

Historically, the industrialized world has operated as a supply-based economy. Specifically, the supply side of the supply/demand equation has driven the balance. It's a model in which companies create products based on a number of factors: maybe the product is likely to make a profit; maybe it's the obvious evolution of the last product; or maybe there is a new ingredient technology that creates differentiation from competitors. Regardless of the driver, traditionally, ideas and plans come from within companies, which then build products in some sort of volume, take them to market and sell them. This is the essence of *push*-driven product development.

The world has always been defined this way. Companies create things. They market them, and they sell them. Some companies may have done a good job of understanding what people want, but the vast majority of product definition lacks the kind of market validation that identifies meaningful customer pull. This is why products fail. How can you hit a target when you don't know where it is?

Things have changed. We now live in a world where user demand is the most important element of the product development equation. Customer/user demand is now the driver of the supply/demand balance. Why? Our technologies, our business processes, our manufacturing processes, and our software creation processes have all advanced to such a degree that it is now possible to make software more effortlessly, create smaller batches of goods and distribute everything more easily. With that, the balance of the supply-and-demand equation is shifting over to consumers.

This is something Burger King started a long time ago: "Have it your way." Now, in the same vein, you can get anything you want at Starbucks, NikeID, and even, increasingly, the local Chevy dealer. There's still a balance in the supply/demand equation, but now customers are in charge. Competition is driving companies to fight even harder to win that customer.

To put emphasis on that point, we're in an economy where, increasingly, successful companies are humbly offering solutions that they believe the customer will want, and validating the demand for those solutions. When companies find a clear signal of demand, they ramp up for it. Going from a supply-based economy to a demand-based economy, where users are in control, requires a new way of thinking about every single aspect of how we conceive, design, develop and take products to market.

As an example, five years ago, we didn't have smart phones and there was no platform for the distribution of the hundreds of thousands of apps that we have today. Now we have a miniaturized supercomputer in our hand that connects to powerful servers in the cloud. Smart phone users can find an app to do most anything they wish and won't download apps they don't want or need. There is absolutely no way to push an app onto a users' phone if they don't desire it. Users are in control of the content they consume and the applications they use more than ever before.

All that leads to the fact that it is almost impossible for companies to push products as they used to. Consumers know they're in charge, and the market driver has gone from supplier/creator-driven push to consumer-driven pull. Customers are seeking out products rather than being pushed or waiting to be marketed to. It's a change that has the deepest of implications.

The market driver flip started during version one of the Internet, which ended with the dot-com crash in the early 2000s. In those early days, the dominant information discovery model was browsing. Yahoo! at that time was essentially just a directory of sites that were relevant to various topics, and users would browse through layer after layer of increasingly more specific categories of websites that were selected by professional web searchers and classifiers. Then a series of search engines came along that were better at supporting users' broad interests. At that point the model changed from discovery based on browsing to discovery based on searching. When users began to feel confident that they could search for—and find—the things they wanted, an economic model of search-based advertising followed. At that point users' online expectations flipped. That's when users no longer took the passive role of waiting to be marketed to online; they went out and found what they wanted for themselves.

The problem Google solved was the creation of a massively scaled system that could meet the most obscure interest of a user and then attach a paying advertiser to that set of search results with a high degree of relevance. For the first time ever, Google provided the capability to match up a user who was searching for a rocket-firing Boba Fett, and connect that person to somebody who sells rare *Star Wars* figures. And Google did it on a scale where even the most obscure user searches created a minimarketplace for connecting buyers and sellers. Before that happened, that person selling the rocket-firing Boba Fett would have never found that buyer and that buyer would have never found that seller. To drive the point home: it's the user's demand for the obscure topic that creates the transaction opportunity, and when the connection is made, everyone wins.

Why Search Is the Perfect Business

Search is the perfect business. Why? Quite simply, it's one of the very few instances of perfect alignment between user intent and the ability of the market to meet that need.

When consumers use a search engine, they express their true intent with the expectation of meeting a need. They aren't shy or bashful about what they may be searching for because it is a request for relevant results. Google is like a magic truth machine. Regardless of whether users are searching for a product or an answer to a question, their search queries represent real, unvarnished intent. That view into users' requests is priceless.

The great thing is there's a market-based way for advertisers to meet that need: advertisers bid for placement in search results and have their performance rated against their success of attracting user clicks through relevance. That's the Google ad model at its simplest. What that means is that the user intent is being matched with a market-driven response from suitors who would like to meet that need.

More often than not, users get exactly what they're expecting. The search results and ads are directly relevant to the query. Contrast that with display adver-

The crux of the problem—and why this book exists—is that in too many cases companies lack either the motivation or ability to adopt a new model for product

tising where ads appear next to online content. Let's say that I'm reading a story about Tiger Woods and a Buick ad appears next to that story. That Buick ad is peripheral to my interest in Tiger Woods; the advertiser seeks to distract me from reading about Tiger. The ad is not the perfect model because I'm there for the content on Tiger Woods, not the Buick.

Furthermore, advertising on the web has become more and more obnoxious. It overlays and obstructs the content of the page. It gets in the way of the reader's attempts to absorb information, and it tries to divert readers to marginally relevant content. Web advertising is a big industry and it works to some degree, but it's far from perfect.

Search, however, is the perfect business. The economics prove it. The revenue per 1,000 searches can easily reach the $100 range. Compare that to traditional advertising rates, say $0.50 to $2.00 per 1,000 page views, and the economics are undeniable. The alignment that user-driven search provides outperforms other advertising models significantly. This is the essence of what it means to tap into user-driven demand, and the same opportunity is available in the creation of products.

creation.[5] The result is that they rely on old ideas about "pushing" products into the market, reflective of the old supply-led balance. Companies that fail to change miss the fantastic opportunity to discover the customer/user/market demand and participate in the resulting superior economics.

As a result, too often products are created and launched into an empty space. For example, there are well over 850,000 apps in the iOS app store. More than 50 percent of those have never had even one download.[6] The problem is that, often, product creators make assumptions about market needs and define products based on vision without truly understanding the state of demand. The result is product launches that lack market acceptance, or even notice.

Yes, there's definitely intuition required to understand what users want. And likewise, there's a high degree of creativity required to understand how to create a product that meets those user needs. But there's also the new requirement that there be humble discovery and

---

5 Ahuja, G. and C. M. Lampert, 2001, "Entrepreneurship in the Large Corporation: A Longitudinal Study of How Established Firms Create Breakthrough Inventions," *Strategic Management Journal* 22, no. 6/7, special issue: Strategic Entrepreneurship: Entrepreneurial Strategies for Wealth Creation: 521– 543

6 Adeven (October 2013), Press Release on Zombie Apps

validation to confirm that the solution is on the right track to meet those needs. This is where the possibility of certainty, measurement and consistent improvement is introduced into the realm of innovation.

The beauty of this is that once those needs are understood, there's less risk of launching into an empty space. It's possible to identify whether customers 1) understand your product, 2) fall in love with it and 3) tell others about it.

CHAPTER THREE

The Need for a New Model

"The health of the eye seems to demand a horizon. We are never tired, so long as we can see far enough."

— RALPH WALDO EMERSON

Real opportunity lies in being the best or most aligned provider of a product or service that meets an emerging market need. Note that I did not say, necessarily, the first to meet the need. The company that combines the discovery of an emerging need with the very best solution to meet that need at scale wins—even if that company is not the one that discovered the need in the first place. The key here is to get a true understanding—the broad perspective as well as the details—of the emerging need and the solution that will best meet that need.

The demand horizon concept tackles the inconvenient fact that seeing beyond the horizon into the unmet needs of your customers is difficult. A simple way to think about it is that user demand tends to start out as a very faint noise. Typically, if enough potential users have a similar need and a similar preference for the way that need is met, a market begins to form. That noise gets a little louder. After that market begins to form, a solution will rise to meet it. Every once in a while some of those needs are so universal that a product really takes off.

Our goal as product creators is to find those signals before they've gelled into a market signal that is so obvious that everyone can hear it. The goal is to be able to look out into this sea of noise and discover what people are looking for in order to be earlier to market and more accurate in meeting that demand.

The diagram on the next page illustrates the three stages of user demand. Imagine user demand as a kind of radio signal that increases and decreases in strength depending on the fit of the product solution. Represented here are the varying degrees of strength and clarity of that demand. Starting all the way to the left at "Potential" (demand), there's not much of a signal at all. The demand density for that signal is very weak. As users become clearer about what they want, that density solidifies into a stronger signal.

At the point when that signal is clear enough to show there's a market, the opportunity crosses the demand horizon—the point where invisibility becomes visibility—and moves from potential demand into current demand. That's where the demand density becomes something identifiable: the market can be described; competitors can be identified; the trajectory and the growth of the market can be estimated, based on reasonable mathematical expectations.

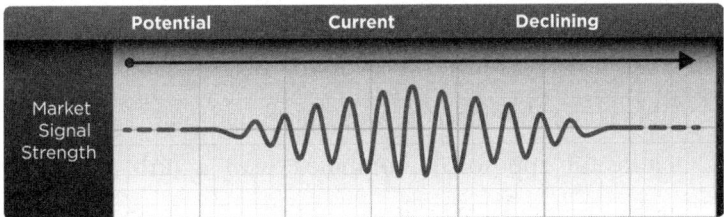

The fundamental idea is that everybody is a market of one. I have my needs and some of them may never be met because they happen to be exclusive to me. As technology advances, however, and as user behavior evolves and people become more sophisticated, those individual needs begin to gel together across many users to form an addressable market.

Take garage-door openers, for example. Just about everybody who has a house has a garage door. And just about everybody carries a phone capable of opening the garage door if the right pieces are put into place. The spark happens when somebody says, "I want to be able to push a button on my phone and open my garage door." If enough people want that, all of a sudden there's a market. The trick lies in being able to spot that market. Where product creators get it really wrong is in assuming that because significant numbers of potential customers have a garage door and a smart phone, they want their phone to automatically open that door. It may be a good idea. It may be a huge mistake. How do you know? You seek to understand user demand.

This is the difference between push and pull. I could create an app today, combined with a little $100 web-connected device that would allow me to open my garage door with my smartphone. I would probably waste a ton of money because there's no signal in the market indicating that people actually want a device to add on to their house to do that. The real question is, out of all the things that people could possibly want, what is happening now and what is going to create a real opportunity? How do I answer that question?

The current approach of creating solutions for a perceived or imagined need is inefficient. It seems obvious, but a lot of money is wasted because companies don't fundamentally understand that they need a rational way to sense demand. There's no awareness of what's actually happening within the potential market.

There are only a few Steve Jobs out there, but there are tens of thousands of passionate, smart product creators who could make better business decisions if they understood how customer demand is discovered and validated.

It immediately becomes clear that a new way of thinking is needed. It's not that all of the old ways are completely wrong. It's just that there are more precise ways to think about the problem of customer demand. Breaking the process of innovation, or product creation, into phases clarifies the innovation opportunity. Seeing demand as a continuum enables more precision in entering or operating in markets.

Welcome to the Demand Economy

It's hard to overestimate the profound effect Geoffrey Moore's *Crossing the Chasm*[7] has had on product development and marketing. I was developing products for the early days of the online world when that book came out. At the time, the web was just a promising idea. Netscape was still in beta and the graphical browser was still very new. We online product managers were all beginning to develop products, but we didn't know exactly how adoption would work. We needed a mental model to enable us to be more precise about what we were doing and to be able to talk intelligently about it.

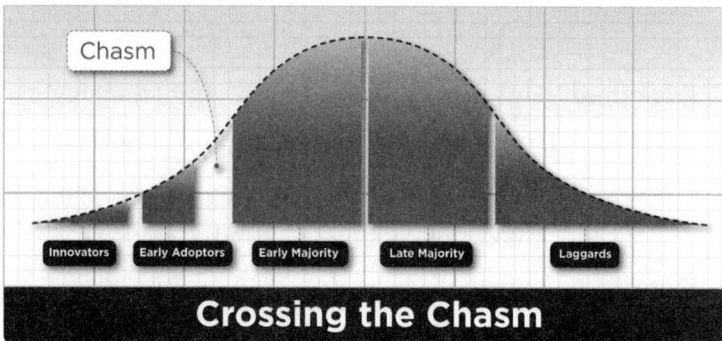

Crossing the Chasm

Geoffrey Moore provided the answer. He took the very old, arcane model explaining the adoption of technology in potato farming and adapted it to the idea of how

---

7 Moore, G. A., 1991, *Crossing the Chasm*, New York: Harper Collins Essentials

technology is adopted and moves through a society. That mental model was the core of *Crossing the Chasm*.

For those of us who were building products at the time, his book was transformational. We now had a way to think about where to gain a beachhead in the market, how to extend that beachhead into the mass market, and how to identify when we had hit the mark.

Product managers and marketers still use the *Chasm* model as the way to describe innovators, early adopters, early majority, and the difficulty of getting word of mouth to achieve mass adoption. That book was pivotal in defining the way we design products on the Internet and now on mobile.

The problem with that approach is that it doesn't go far enough into the critical determinant of success: consumer demand. We can understand exactly what the stages of adoption are and we can describe the systematic passage from one market definition to the next. However, to truly understand the system, we need to go deeper. We need to look at the actual source of momentum. We need to look at, and understand, the core driver of the emergence of new products and the motivations of people who pony up money to buy them.

To understand what makes great products, how the break-out successes happen, we need to isolate the idea of consumer demand and understand the subtleties of pushing a product into the market versus tapping into and cultivating market pull.

In the previous time, when supply drove the balance between supply and demand, there was limited ability to create and distribute products and manufacturers had the benefit of scarcity. Because Henry Ford was one of the few car manufacturers of his day, he could give customers all of the colors they desired—as long as they wanted black.

Today, creation and distribution of cars has reached maturity, and there are enough manufacturers seeking out user needs in the marketplace. Consumers have a multitude of choices—red ones, green ones, convertibles—and all from a large range of brands and in every imaginable size and configuration. Have you shopped for an SUV lately? Any idea why the same company often offers two or three different mid-sized SUVs? Consumers are now able to define what they want and car makers are responding.

The same thing has happened with online products. It has become very easy to create new software, Internet and mobile products. We've got decades and decades of computer platform development and off-the-shelf-component software that make it easy and just about free for companies to create new product solutions. That opens up a lot of choices.

Along with that proliferation of products, it has also become comparatively simple to distribute anything, whether over the Internet or by highly developed physical distribution services such as Fedex. We have created the perception of unlimited supply, so now demand is driving the supply/demand balance. The user is in control. In turn, we now have to create a new model for understanding that user demand.

To be fair to Geoffrey Moore, the product adoption curve in *Crossing the Chasm* still applies once a product has been defined and is ready to go to market. But how do product managers determine what to build? We are now—in terms of sophistication—in a world that is very primitive in terms of sensing demand and figuring out what type of products to create.

The demand-based economy ultimately arises out of the proliferation of choice and the ability to create and distribute products—whether physical products or software products—very cheaply and easily. And consumer expectations are demanding.

As users, we expect relevance in our search results and our search advertising. We expect to be able to choose not just the model and color of car but the size of engine, the type of sound system, and so on. We expect to be able to choose everything from the countertops in our house to the people we interact with online. It's a completely new phase of the economy.

Successful product creation, whether it's hard goods or software, will be driven by our ability to determine and build, accurately and efficiently, what users want. Ultimately, there are a couple of layers of relevant questions. Has the market expressed a need for something that has yet to be created? What form does that need take? Exactly what product features are going to be the ones that win the most favor? How big is the market? We need answers to these questions and with those answers we'll be able to increase certainty around new product creation.

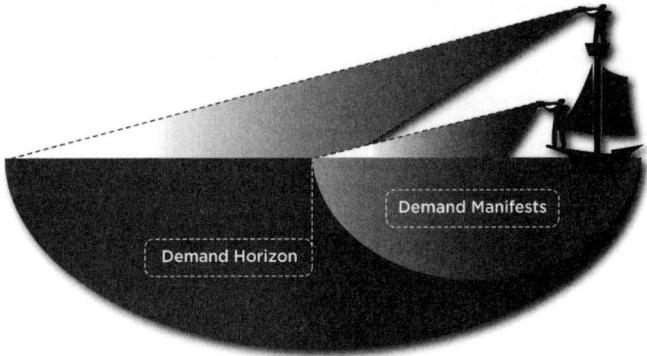

Demand Manifests

Demand Horizon

Why Is There a Demand Horizon?

Market demand follows the same pattern as the visible horizon. The story of the telescope is a good analogy. The telescope was invented around the early 1600s. People used it almost immediately for astronomy and warfare, to be able to see long-distance, study stars and prepare for battle. It wasn't until almost 50 years later that someone decided to put one on a ship, with the idea of using it to spot things that couldn't normally be seen with the eye.

Almost unbelievably, it wasn't until 1807 that a British explorer strapped a pickle barrel to the top of the mast and created the first crow's nest. At that point, some 150 years after telescopes were initially taken to sea, some seafarer figured out that he could sit at the top of

51

the mast with one to see what was beyond the horizon. By taking existing technology and using it in a creative way, it was possible to see farther into the great beyond, increasing certainty in navigation and warfare.

This is an exact parallel to what's going on today. Unaided it is difficult—even impossible—to sense user demand. But with the tools of data analysis and directed research it's possible to see much farther into the land beyond the demand horizon. We now have the telescope but haven't climbed the mast yet. Big data has given us the perspective. The details

> We want to decrease cost, increase the likelihood of success of new product launches, and take the guesswork out of the process.

companies have on users and their usage is amazing, but it's one thing to have access to data; it's quite another to understand it.

We sit in a murky world right now. We have data, which is the potential, and we've got the tools. Now it's just a matter of strapping the pickle barrel to the top of the mast and pulling out the telescope. We've got all the pieces we need; we just have to use them.

The promise of using this approach is that it is possible to improve the success rate of product launches dramatically. By taking the right perspective and conducting the right analysis prior to release, products can be launched into a market without having to wonder whether there is demand. Instead, you'll already have a really good idea of exactly which product configuration will work and exactly where the users are who will find value in the product.

By defining products to meet specific identified and quantified demand, market launch is not initiated until there is at least a preliminary understanding of configuration. It leads to less risk in launching new products. It leads to higher success rates. All of this equates to a more efficient business and better margins. We want to decrease cost, increase the likelihood of success of new product launches, and take the guesswork out of the process.

CHAPTER FOUR

The Demand Horizon

"We're not in the business of shaping consumer demand. We respond to it."

— STEVE LARGENT

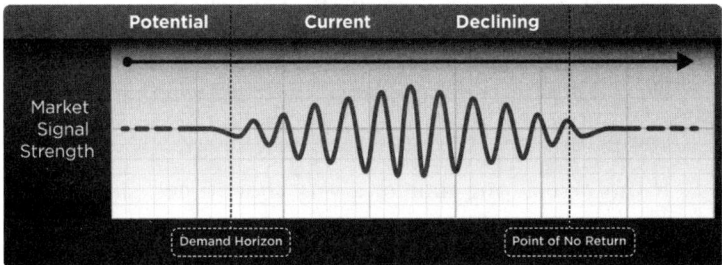

Users make very quick decisions about what they do and don't want to buy. Success is defined not only by whether or not *customers* adopt a product but also by whether or not they tell *other people* about it and convince them to adopt it. In order to be able to succeed within that demand-driven model, we need to break product creation down in a way that allows us to take action at the various points of user interest. This will enable a precise understanding of how to optimize product/market fit.

What I mean, very specifically, is that user demand evolves. Each stage requires a different set of strategies and tactics. At first, potential users just have an inkling that they need a solution, but they can't articulate it. That inkling gets a little stronger over time, so there comes a point when people can articulate what they need, but they're not positive about what form the solution should take. After that, the time comes when it's very clear what they need. Ultimately, the time comes when their need has been met and their demand for a solution shifts to something else, whether it's a competitor, a substitute, a new technology, and so on. It can take a long time or a very short time. Lately, it seems that time cycle is getting shorter by the day.

What we've described here is a continuum that starts with vague market demand. For instance, people may or may not know they need a new app to help them stay in touch with their loved ones. Ultimately, it becomes very clear that they need that app because their loved ones are using it and they're missing out. After that, they may get bored with it and move on to some other solution. That's the essence of what we're trying to capture with this model. We can break the process down into phases of demand to understand that user demand is the basis of product creation.

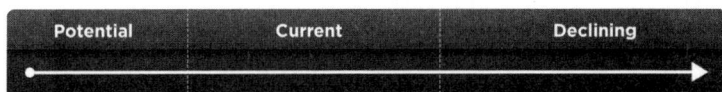

Potential	Current	Declining

The Three Stages of Demand

As it evolves, user demand tends to follow a pattern of change through three distinct stages. Before we drill down deep to understand how to best take advantage of each stage, let's just briefly take a high-level view of each one.

Potential Demand

Potential demand is an untapped opportunity. There are a few reasons why it is untapped. One is that there's no solidification of need, so it's something that's new, something that has yet to be visualized or delivered; a need exists but there's no real solution yet. This is where true innovation lies.

Matching up that need with a solution is really difficult because consumers don't know how to ask for things that don't exist. Very few people sit around imagining new products. If users don't know a product exists, they can't articulate it. It's very difficult to create something for a market that can't articulate the solution that will work for its need. Potential demand often is just this bound-up situation in which people have a need they can't articulate.

The reason for this is the gap between thought and behavior.[8] When people try to verbally express what they want, their description is usually very different from what would be revealed through their actual behavior. To identify needs, demand must be explored in a nonstandard way.

Current Demand

Current demand is what is seen in existing markets every day: there are buyers, sellers and market equilibrium. In this stage of demand there is a known market and there is some understanding of how the market operates. Interestingly, this is the stage of demand most covered in the academic and popular business press.

---

8 Samuelson, P. A., 1948, "Consumption Theory in Terms of Revealed Preference," *Economica,* New Series 15, no. 60: 243–253.

Porter's five forces, the sales/marketing funnel, SWOT analysis and nearly everything anyone ever learned in business school falls within this range. Classical strategy and competition models all deal with a certain set of known variables—primarily, the existence of a known market.

Declining Demand

Declining demand is just what it sounds like. It's the stage when the market that once was alive and growing is now suffering from decreasing users, usage, sales or profit. The interesting issue is that, as managers, humans tend to be slow to identify, acknowledge or act on the decline of products.[9] Whether it's because of institutional inertia—salaried employees continuing out of a sense of duty and/or job justification—or a lack of awareness, the objective recognition that a business is in decline presents interesting and often very profitable opportunities.

Recognition is often slow and actions are frequently too small to prevent the decline. With a clear understanding of the demand cycle, it becomes easier to identify, diagnose and act on a declining business.

---

9 Sinkula, J. M., 1994, "Market Information Processing and Organizational Learning," *Journal of Marketing* 58 (January): 35–45

The term *certainty* has been used to describe the goal in effective demand management, and that doesn't just mean certainty of success. In the case of decline, certainties of decrease are thrust on the product and management teams. By recognizing this situation and acting with decisiveness, the resulting actions of closing/divesting/reinventing can be just as strategic and innovative as earlier stages in the continuum.

A Closer Look

Potential demand is the biggest challenge. This is where true invention lies. Nobody knew they needed a tablet device before the iPad came along. It was a completely unproven concept to think that people had a desire to carry around a computing device that would allow them to do so many different things. In fact, previous attempts, such as the ill-fated Apple Newton, had failed miserably, but Steve Jobs stuck to the idea. He happened to understand that people would want certain capabilities via computing. How did he understand that? He had a great concept of trends and he also had the ability to shape and create desirable products. Nevertheless, there was a point in time when nobody knew they wanted an iPad. Now every device has a big screen and runs apps.

Potential demand is elusive. Until its existence has been confirmed by market adoption of a real product solution, one has to go on either blind exploration, or superior navigation capabilities. The very definition of potential is that it's got stored energy. Potential energy is sitting in the market. A need has developed and it's on the verge of finding a voice.

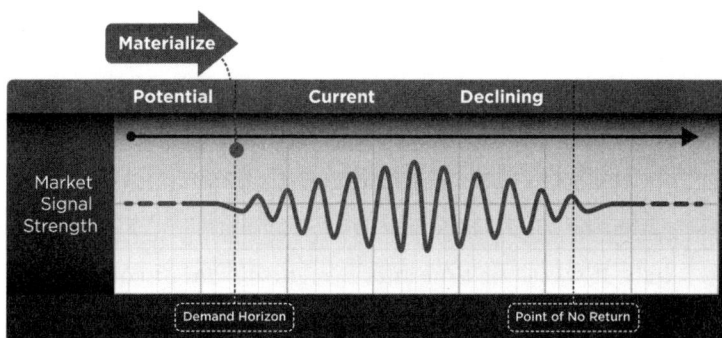

Breakthrough products tap into this potential energy with surprising frequency. It's not a rare event. For instance, just 30 years ago carrying a mobile phone was something out of *Star Trek*; our suitcases didn't all have wheels; we listened to music on cassette tapes; a TV was large if it had a 30-inch screen; and nobody had ever seen a bottle opener/flip flop. The list of innovations that have changed our lives is nearly infinite, and with each one of them came transformational business opportunities for those involved. It's very easy to under-estimate how our lives have changed, and to discount the possibility of creating new, impactful breakthroughs today.

As product creators and inventors, our aspiration is to meet a need with mass appeal, providing a solution for the broadest number of people in the most profitable way. Often solutions are only obvious *after* they have been provided.

A great illustration is the proverbial egg of Columbus.[10] As the story goes, Christopher Columbus was at a gathering of intellectuals and explorers in Florence, Italy. It was some time after his return from discovering America, and there were those who doubted the signif-icance of the discovery. In fact, there were those who claimed finding America was unremarkable because of the obviousness of it. In reply, Columbus challenged the men around the table to make an egg stand on its end. Each one tried, using every imaginable way to balance the egg. All failed, claiming it couldn't be done. Ultimately, they stopped trying. Columbus took the egg, tapped the bottom to create a flat spot, and the egg stood solidly upright. The solution is obvious

10 Girolamo Benzoni [1565] 2001, *History of the New World*, Boston: Adamant Media Corporation

when you already know it. That is exactly what it's like to discover a meaningful source of potential demand, pushing through uncertainty to find a solution.

Invention of Search Box Suggestions: My Experience in Discovering Potential Demand

There was a time when it was very, very hard to find relevant information on the Internet. The volume of content available to the average user was exploding at a previously unimagined rate. The compound problem we—as a team tasked with building information products—had at AOL was that 1) users were not confident or sophisticated enough to find information for themselves, and 2) the technology had not been built to empower users to navigate the vast seas of information effectively. Many things we think of as being obvious solutions had not been thought of at that time.

The proverbial egg didn't have a flat spot yet. Someone had to solve the riddles.

In 2002, as GM of AOL Search, I would routinely pull engineers, product managers, designers and business intelligence people together to explore and create. With a whiteboard and data we would ponder the future possibilities of user experience and technology. This exploration time has turned out to be one of my most fruitful and cherished experiences of my career. Creative collaboration is one of the most rewarding things I believe humans can do. To tie it to demand-horizon terms, we would pick up the tools of creativity and data analysis, climb up to the crow's nest and try to peer beyond the visible horizon into the things users couldn't yet articulate they wanted, into the potential demand. Sometimes nothing would come out of these meetings, and sometimes we'd generate interesting solutions. Those solutions would be written up and sent to the intellectual property attorneys to see if there was anything unique enough to apply for a patent. Often enough there was.

One particular day I was looking at a frustrating fact in the data: 30 percent of the time, after searching, users would try another query rather than clicking into the page containing the results of their search. When they did click, often it was far down the page, deep into the list of results. What did this mean? That for a very large portion of the time users were struggling to find what they were looking for. They had to search again, scan a lot of results, scroll down the page—all indicators that the experience could have been better. It was a known problem, and a whole industry was trying to deal with it by making the search results themselves more relevant, but for some reason I wasn't satisfied and that was the day to do something about it.

Lara Mehanna, who was in charge of product management, joined me in my office and we began to go over what we knew. We pulled out our usage reports, and we scoured what we had learned from conversations with users, usability sessions and business intelligence reports from previous product tests. The goal was to isolate the *real* need, the *real* user challenge. Our answer? People didn't actually know what they were looking for, or were not sophisticated enough in their searches to ask with precision. How can you supply a great set of search results when users aren't expressing their needs with clarity?

This led to the first insight: Search entry boxes are about questions. Search results pages are about answers. Don't solve the question problem in the answer environment. Solve it in the question environment! The search entry box! The next thing we did was look at all of the various types of searches in the query stream: Sometimes people search for things with addresses. So they probably want a map. Sometimes they search for websites, with a .com or .net address, so they are looking for a website. Before too long we had a concise list of possibilities. So we needed to create a search entry box that was intelligent enough to look at the query *as the user was typing* and make suggestions about what might be relevant. There was nothing like it out in the market, and data suggested that, if it could be built, it might go a long way to improving the confidence and accuracy of a user's search.

But could it be built? Lara picked up the phone and called superengineer Herman Vandermolen to help figure it out. He and his team member Shawkat Hasan, after a lot of prototyping, thinking and testing, nailed it. Throughout the process there were many, many challenges. Even more difficult to overcome than the technical difficulties were the voices that said it was impossible to make it work quickly enough to feel natural, or too computationally expensive to implement without driving operational costs too high. But we could see that the power this could put into the users' hands was transformational. It would make users significantly more effective in their searching.

Eventually, the SmartBox was launched. The functionality worked exactly as designed, and we saw immediate improvement in single-search sessions and more clicking at the top of the search results page. Success. The patents were applied for, and we went back to running a search engine.

Funny thing, though. The idea took root—in a huge way. The Columbus' egg of search box suggestions had a flat spot now and the idea was in use all over the web.

By my estimation, given that every major search, social networking site, mobile device and Internet appliance uses predictive search suggestions, about 30 percent of the world's seven billion people use the technology. You don't know it as predictive search, or SmartBox. You know it as that thing that pops down and helps you search. It's used by Google, Facebook, Android, Apple, as well as nearly every web site and mobile device on the planet. It has become so ubiquitous in the last 10 years that I had almost forgotten about that project back at AOL, and I had certainly doubted the assertion that we were first to market with it. In August 2011 the patent was granted, recognizing our team of horizon explorers as the originators of the technology. Since then it has been sold to Facebook as a strong part of its patent portfolio.

As proud of that team and our technology as I am, that's not the point of the story. The point is that the demand-horizon approach is powerful. Its power comes from a few simple points:

- Users and customers are calling the shots now; demand drives innovation; and companies that recognize that are more likely to succeed.

- It is possible with the right approach, one that trades ego and vision for humility and user-driven exploration, to tap into that demand.

- Demand plays a part at every stage of business, and by recognizing your current stage, it's possible to craft effective strategy and supporting tactics.

- Through application of the demand-horizon mental model, it's possible to get superior economics and achieve scale beyond your wildest imagination.

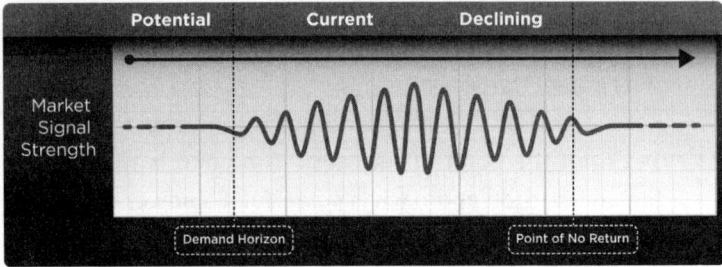

Becoming a Taste Maker

During the early stage of potential demand it's very difficult to see the stored-up energy. But ultimately, that energy becomes very clear. That is where the demand horizon lies. It's right at that edge between the time when people don't know how to express what they want and the time when their demand begins to gel into something recognizable. The moment that demand solidifies, it becomes time to scale that market.

Once potential demand becomes something that can be seen, understood, and predicted, it has moved into the visible horizon. The demand horizon lies in that transition between potential demand and current demand.

Companies that can see that demand before it solidifies are the ones that get first-mover advantage. They're the ones that have the ability to shape the market. In the best-case scenario, they have the chance to shape the market in a way that suits their business and meets the needs of their customers. They become the taste makers.

....

Case Study: When Push Fails

Ever since agile and lean development swept through the tech industry nearly a decade ago, "getting out of the building" and talking to potential customers has been a cornerstone of new product development. However, it is rarely done, and when it is done it is often conducted incorrectly. Why? Because talking to people about your product is hard and painful. However this is a critical activity for understanding potential demand.

The best technology companies are capable of routinely testing their new products, even secretly, with their core users and absorbing feedback. Microsoft, however, has for years and for scores of products failed to show strength in prelaunch product validation.

Often after companies reach out to the general public for product guidance, indications are that the feedback was not factored into product development: the companies stayed the course despite clear negative feedback—to predictable and widely documented results.

During the launch of the Kin, Steve Ballmer's $1 billion next-generation smart phone program, the development team did have the foresight to put the new devices in the hands of consumers. Unfortunately, by that time the phones were all but built and any major course corrections were out of the question. And what did people think?

They hated them.

Prelaunch comments included, "It's frustrating. I can imagine my daughter would give this back very quickly," and "It just can't quite keep up," when referencing the operating system's time lag. Despite the substantive and clear feedback, Microsoft proceeded to launch with its partner, Verizon. The phones were pulled from the shelves after 48 days.

The recent Surface debacle is no brighter a tale. Much is the same for Windows 8. Perhaps this should not be surprising given Ballmer's views on product development: "I like to tell people that all of our products and business will go through three phases. There's vision, patience, and execution." Not a lot of room there for testing or market validation.

Gaining unbiased user feedback is central to product development now. No longer can products be built purely by gut instinct and then pushed onto the market. Users must be involved, and listened to, from the moment development begins. To ignore your users is to court failure.

Avoiding this failure is as simple (and devilishly complicated) as setting up routine, lightweight and low-risk conversations with your future customers. But as we have seen, it is not enough to merely talk to your users; you must actually listen to their feedback and take action to resolve any problems they identify. Creating products with your customers is the real state of the art.

....

CHAPTER FIVE

Exploring Potential Demand

"If advertisers spent the same amount of money on improving their products as they do on advertising, then they wouldn't have to advertise them.

—WILL ROGERS

How exactly do we explore, test and discover potential demand? Here's a way to think about it: Imagine any type of noisy marketplace. You can visualize a medieval market complete with wooden carts, chickens running around, and lots of noisy people, or envision a commodities trading floor with brokers screaming and yelling and holding up strips of paper. In general, our current marketplace is not much different from either of those examples. They are all noisy and people are engaged in a nearly infinite number of activities—chaos.

From within all of that noise and energy, occasionally, a seeming organization of sounds can arise, such as a particularly loud, synchronized group clapping in unison to a musician. Or the noise may be a single shout heard above the crowd that causes the din to subside for a few moments while market goers pay attention. Sometimes the commotions are small. Sometimes the entire market pays attention and participates. Spotting demand is analogous to sensing and responding to these brief and unpredictable moments.

So, getting back to the real world of business, why do these moments of synchronized attention happen? There are three reasons: The first is the introduction of new elemental technology—essentially improvements in the raw materials that things are made of. Maybe it's a new understanding of how plastics work, a new technique for creating metals, or a new way to use silicon. All of these things are pushing the materials in our world forward, making possible the new capabilities that are being constantly introduced to us.

The second reason for progression is new connective technologies. These are the things that allow us to communicate, to learn, to gather information, to buy and sell, and to synthesize ideas—the things that help people transfer information, conduct transactions and access entertainment. They have all undergone massive improvements in the past decade and are in the process of progressing even further. You can't hide from them.

The third reason is simply an ever-progressing sophistication in how humans meet their basic needs. These underlying basic needs never change in their fundamental form; it is their expression that changes.

As users' experience of the world evolves, they are constantly exposed to new technologies, new ways of doing things, new ways of connecting to each other, and new ways of learning. Every day there are new opportunities to change the way we have traditionally done things.

With something new being introduced every day, it becomes very difficult to understand what the next new thing will be and how to get the timing right. The way to do that is not to ask people what they want, because they just can't articulate it. It's impossible to get users to describe a solution they have never seen or used before. It is possible, however, to take a look at the way targeted users currently behave and to study their attitudes to obtain very specific clues to how to improve their effectiveness, efficiency or entertainment value.

Where to Look for a Demand Signal

TOOL #1: QUERY STREAM

Long before Google existed, I was working in product management at AltaVista, creating new online shopping and advertising products. I had access to usage patterns and could study how users expressed their needs in the aggregate stream of all search queries. We could learn so much by looking at how people interacted with the page, what they clicked on, how their eyes traveled over the expanse of the search results. It was particularly exciting considering that, as we've already established, the economy is now driven by what people want, not necessarily by what we want to push on them.

A search engine is such a powerful tool because it is a place where users come to express exactly what they want in the form of a query. People come in looking for solutions to their problems, fulfillment of their needs, and an end to their frustration. All of that is expressed in a search engine query box. It's got every possible human desire; some good, some bad, some beautiful and some very ugly. It's all in there.

The ability to see into the collective user mind through that query stream transformed my understanding of how to create and validate new product ideas. Being able to comb through search data is amazingly powerful. It's a little bit tricky to get to that data if you don't own or manage a search engine, but it's not impossible. The broad range of analytic tools can be found by searching for "SEM tools" on your favorite search engine. It is amazing what kinds of information can be learned about how people search, where they click, and how they think of you and your competitors. These tools were designed to help marketers understand how to buy advertising more effectively, but we can take that exact same data, look at it with a different focus and get fantastic insight into real user demand. This is what is meant by taking the telescope up to the crow's nest to get a better view past the horizon. As an industry we've had this data for a while, but very few products are built based on the insights we can gather from looking into it.

There are a number of other tools out there that are designed for search-engine marketers and search-engine optimizers and enable exploration into what people are searching for. We have an unbelievable amount of data available. With the right query-exploration tools it is possible to get a deep understanding of the way your potential audience is voicing user demand.

Are potential users searching for things in a generic sense? Are they looking for alternatives to existing products? Are they complaining about a lack of features on a certain product? All of those things, when trended over time, allow you to come up with a picture of whether something is actually starting to move from potential demand into a current-demand situation.

With traditional market research it is possible to spend tens of thousands of dollars on a single product studying what target users say they like, what they don't like, and whether the proposed product will meet their needs. Unfortunately, the correlation between what people *say* and what they *do* is very low.[11] Often this gives false signals.

If you understand what people are doing and how they think by the way they search, you can begin to understand not just whether there is a market opportunity but which features are the most important.

---

11 Samuelson, P. A., 1948, "Consumption Theory in Terms of Revealed Preference," *Economica, New Series* 15, no. 60: 243–253

TOOL #2: USER CONVERSATIONS

Another powerful tool is to conduct user conversations. Gather spontaneous and candid feedback by interviewing potential users and, whenever possible, showing a visual mockup, prototype, or the real product. It may seem obvious to do this, but remember Columbus. What is not obvious is that, in this case, you're asking users to give their reactions to a very specific thing. The power comes in not just what you're testing but how you interpret the response. Look at their emotion: their tone of voice, their level of excitement, the movement of their eyes and eyebrows. You're looking for the fleeting reaction that will never show up in a market research report. The key is to observe whether they understand the product's value proposition and are excited to have their needs met in that particular way. It's almost an anthropological task rather than a market research task. You're not specifically asking, "Will you like this or will you not? Will you use this or not? Do you have this need or not?" What you're seeing is a need that has not been expressed. Market research gives you expressed needs. Observation of users in a conversation enables a deeper understanding.

TOOL #3: OBSERVATION

A third way to get insights about user demand is by looking at data usage patterns. This technique is all about big data and business intelligence. Those who are fortunate enough to have a website with established traffic already have usage data. In this data it's possible to see how people are moving through the site, what pages they enter, which pages they leave, and so on.

If it is possible to get relevant usage data, study it to see what features, pages and capabilities users are frequenting. How deeply are they going? How long are they staying? If it is possible to observe behavior patterns, do so. Don't ask users what they're doing. Go observe it. If you want to launch a new laundry detergent, go watch how people select laundry detergent. If you want to launch a new bicycle, go watch how consumers buy bicycles in stores. Don't ask them how they do it. Watch how they do it.

Now, there's a little bit of a challenge built into this. There's a law in physics that states, "As soon as you observe something, it changes." The act of observing something changes it, but if you're observing it in retrospect and looking at data, that's not a concern. Minimizing the awareness or impact of observation is a good thing.

This is the promise of big data. In a world where companies are gathering and making available all kinds of data about what people actually do, the most arcane little details can be the key to spotting user demand. This is where the ability to gather large volumes of data becomes really interesting.

TOOL #4: COMPETITIVE ANALYSIS

Traditional competitive analysis looks at feature match-ups, comparative strengths and weaknesses, distribution strategies and pricing. Those measures are appropriate when looking at the competition within a known, or current, market. But what about competitive analysis in unknown markets where there is just potential demand? It seems counterintuitive that competitive analysis brings any insight into a situation that, by definition, has no direct competitors. But competitive analysis is critical. Here's why: instead of looking for direct match-ups and head-to-head competitors, the goal is to look for indicators in the activities of the market that signal demand.

There are three key dimensions of competitive analysis for potential demand:

- **Others seeking a similar demand signal:** Have other companies tried to identify and isolate the same demand signal you see? How well did they do? Where did they pivot, and into what?

- **Indicator of the status of the demand:** Is there an acceleration of companies seeking to meet similar opportunities? Deceleration? What sort of timing was there and how has the market environment changed?

- **Adjacent demand:** Does it look as if any other company in a business related to yours is finding fertile ground? Is there insight to be gained from looking at related needs?

By exploring the activity of other companies seeking to meet similar and related forms of demand, it becomes possible to get a complete landscape of the environment where the new product will potentially resonate.

The Eight-Second Rule

In exploring potential demand, we know it's very hard for people to articulate what they want. It's difficult to know exactly what solutions the potential market is seeking. This is where the eight-second rule is valuable. It's based on data regarding how long visitors stay on websites before they bounce out, how much attention is given to mobile apps and a significant amount of direct testing.[12]

It comes down to a very simple idea: when introducing a new product, you have eight seconds to hook someone. Remember, it's a very noisy market and there are countless things competing for the consumer's attention. To determine if your new product is hitting potential demand, all you have is eight seconds.

This is a good rule of thumb for getting that cursory validation that a concept, prototype or alpha product meets some existing user demand. Why eight seconds? In the first four seconds the goal is to validate understanding of the value proposition. "Here's a concept. Here's an idea. Do you understand it? Does it make sense to you?"

That's the beginning of the eight-second rule. You show people something; you talk about it. For instance, you show a mock-up of a website and ask, "Do you know what this website does? Do you know what this app does?"

If your prospective users look at the page and confirm they understand what it does, you've got the first part of the eight seconds. The next part of the eight seconds

---

12 Oulasvirta, A., S. Tamminen, V. Roto, and J. Kuorelahti, 2005, "Interaction in 4-Second Bursts: The Fragmented Nature of Attentional Resources in Mobile HCI," *Proceedings on the SIGCHI Conference on Human Factors in Computing Systems,* 919–928

is figuring out if those people love it and if it taps into something they really need.

After the first four seconds when it is confirmed that prospective users understand your product, the next four seconds will tell you if you really have that spark. It doesn't happen very often, but if you can get a user to look at something and say, "Yes, this is something that I need to have," and you see the excitement or engagement in that person's face, you'll know you have the spark.

The bar is high. It's difficult to create a product that is both understood and loved in eight seconds. However, it's the required validation to identify whether your solution has isolated and addressed a source of demand. The first four seconds tests the product's message for clarity and positioning. If you get it right, you're on track to alignment and good brand resonance. If prospects don't understand your product in the first four seconds, you should stop until you get that right and continue to

....

Case Study: The Eight-Second Rule, Part One—What Is It?

In 2010 the whole tech world was abuzz with Facebook's global reach and newcomer Instagram's meteoric rise. Media sharing was king and investors could not get enough of these companies. Enter Bill Nguyen, an iterate. Again, certainty takes many forms. If you have certainty that the product does not yet resonate, that is extremely helpful. Acknowledge it. Keep trying. If you proceed past this phase without the prospective user immediately understanding your offering, there is not just risk but near certainty that time, money and effort will be wasted.

Once you achieve consistent, positive recognition of your product in the first four seconds, you move on to the next four seconds, which are more elusive. The idea is that the value proposition needs to meet with a spark of demand. You've got to have that spark, because that's a required element to drive word of mouth.

That's the goal. Prospective users have to know what the product is and they have to love it in order to generate word-of-mouth promotion. As we set out to understand potential demand, that signal that we're looking for—the thing we are trying to attach to—lies in that spark of excitement.

entrepreneur with a proven track-record of launching and selling companies for high dollar amounts, his latest success being a music streaming site to Apple to the tune of $80 million.

Sensing the frothiness of the market but lacking any concrete ideas, Nguyen gathered together six smart engineers in a 22,000-square-foot storefront and went calling on venture capitalists. That netted him $13 million from Bain Capital and Silicon Valley Bank.

The product they eventually came up with was a photo-sharing social network that was built around proximity. Rather than "friending" other people, you instead took photos of your life, which in turn showed up on the feeds of other users who were within 150 feet of you. This was supposed to create "flash communities" and foster connections. Along the way the company bought the URLs color.com, for $350,000, and colour.com, for $75,000, as well as hiring 30 more employees and two high-profile executives. Peter Pham of Photobucket and D. J. Patil of LinkedIn were named president and head of product respectively.

After all this, the team hit tech press heavily. From New York City to San Francisco, they hyped up Color and showed off the app to the influential. Finally, they began discussions with Sequoia Capital that quickly netted them another $28 million, for a total of $41 million—before launch.

When the launch did come in 2011, it did not go smoothly. No one, from bloggers to average users understood what Color was or how it worked. Onboarding screens were sparse and icons were not intuitive. Worst of all, because the app was proximity based, initial users were greeted with blank screens that were supposed to be filled with others' pictures. A key feature of the product, the ability to see others' photos, didn't work because Color users were not close enough to each other for the proximity algorithms to find pictures nearby.

The Color team quickly added a disclaimer to the app store, "WARNING: DON'T USE COLOR ALONE." Despite this, the average rating for the app was a deathly two stars. In the end, Color garnered 400,000 monthly active users. By contrast, at the time, Instagram had seven million daily active users. Despite their massive bankroll, Color officially shut its doors in late 2012.

Even though the team had an impressive track record of exits, and were all A-class talent, they collectively failed at vaulting the first hurdle of product creation: making something that the consumer understands. Much of the negative feedback received through the app store centered on basic navigation confusion and design elements. Color did not pass the first four seconds of the eight-second rule: consumers could not understand what the app was or what it did. Employees of Color have since admitted that user testing only extended to the team itself and the firm's investors. Just before launch, the tech blogging community roundly panned the app's confusing design and layout, yet the app was still released. By testing with real potential users, the development team could have not just saved itself a headache but saved the entire company as well.

You must test. Fake a design in PowerPoint, create web mocks, paint a picture, or use pencil and paper if you have to. Design, test, redesign, and keep testing until eight out of every ten people can tell you immediately what your product does.

Consumer product success is not determined by whether you have a successful track record. Nor is it enough to have a truckload of funding. Even surrounding yourself with the best talent can't guarantee success. You need to make something that obviously and plainly showcases its purpose and benefit immediately.

....

Case Study: Eight-Second Rule, Part Two—Do They Love it?

After about 30 years in dormancy, in 2009, 3-D movie making was thrust back into the consumer market with the release of *Avatar*. From that point 3-D-enabling technology surged to popularity in movie theaters.

Additionally, a long list of manufacturers were offering the enhancement for use in homes via 3-D TVs. James Cameron, Stephen Spielberg and a host of entertainment pioneers were staking out claims to the perceived opportunity, including the patents behind it. All of the technologies were exploding and there was froth in consumer electronics marketing commensurate with the beginning of a massive trend.

In 2011 phone manufacturers interpreted this market boom as a signal that the 3-D trend would continue its march from the big screen to the 45-inch screen on the wall to the 3.5-inch screen in hundreds and hundreds of millions of smartphone-toting hands. The opportunity to grab that market and be the provider of the first/best 3-D phone was irresistible to companies such as HTC, Sprint and LG. The technology was available to make a phone display three dimensional. In fact, to spark excitement even more, the phones had revolutionary screens that didn't require the user to wear glasses. The 3-D effect could be seen with the unaided eye. The perfect storm: enabling technology, content, a willing market …

Wait! Was the market really willing? The answer was no. Within the first month Sprint cut the price of the Evo 3-D from $549.99 to $199.99 to stimulate sales, and the phones still clogged up the store shelves. It might have been a question regarding timing, as Sprint claimed, but my suspicion is that there were more fundamental issues around users' willingness to adopt an entertainment technology in their daily, utility-driven lives. Regardless, this was a massive misinterpretation of potential demand.

In post launch-and-fail interviews several execs commented on their surprise at the flop. They cited scores of tech bloggers and influencer interviews reinforcing excitement about the new phones. They alluded to market research that validated market acceptance. So, the critical question: could it have been avoided? Absolutely.

3-D phones fall completely flat on the eight-second rule.

The phones passed the first part of the test. The technology isn't difficult to understand; 3-D was everywhere. It was not a difficult leap to comprehend a hand-held device displaying things in that way. And the key drawback of 3-D movies and TVs was addressed: no glasses needed. That was certainly easy to understand. I am quite sure there would be no issue with the first four seconds.

But that next four seconds was the killer: Did people love it? Definitely not.

Had Sprint, HTC or LG simply walked out to a busy street corner in Los Angeles, New York City or Middle America and shown the phone to 10 people, it's easy to guess in retrospect what the answer would have been. In fact, by reading the blogs, you can see that there was immediate negative reaction, leading to the price drops and eventual failure: the screen was darker; the 3-D camera made the device bigger; battery life suffered. Those three problems decreased the perceived utility of the devices below a critical level. Clearly it was a no-go. Some simple prototyping and user testing would have saved hundreds of millions of dollars in development, manufacturing and marketing.

What can we learn from this? First of all, technical capabilities can often progress past market demand. Building products based on the availability of technology can lead to very expensive mistakes. Second, trends exposing demand for comparable products (in this case 3-D movies and TV) can lead to misinterpretation. Trends can give us clues, but are insufficient for identifying real opportunity. Third, customers have the first and the last say. Ask what they want, create it, and then use the eight-second rule to validate that you've hit the right product for the market. If you miss, learn and try again. Going back to the drawing board is time consuming and painful, but less so than an expensive mass failure.

....

Why Traditional Market Research Is Inadequate

Most often research asks subjects to state their preferences: "Do you like this? Do you like that? What do you think about that idea? Do you do this or that, and how often …" Whether the study is quantitative or qualitative, when you ask people to rank their attitudes and preferences, or ask them to report their behaviors, you're engaging the part of their brain that is considering, contemplating and processing the question being asked. Research about stated versus revealed preferences shows that there is a weak relationship between people's responses to research questions and real behavior.[13] In fact, their responses are mostly about how they see themselves or how they want to be seen by others. That's not helpful in understanding whether there is a market for your product. Remember, when they're at the stage

---

13 Samuelson, P. A., 1948, "Consumption Theory in Terms of Revealed Preference," *Economica, New Series* 15, no. 60: 243–253

of potential demand where there is no readily apparent solution for the need, people can't state what they want.

This reliance on traditional market research is one of the biggest problems in product development. Companies tend to make decisions based on what can be measured with traditional methods, which is in the current demand range. Management understands operating metrics and financials. These are not available while you're exploring potential demand for a new market opportunity, since the demand signal is emerging and not solidified. Don't fall for the false security of market research just because it makes the story easier to tell.

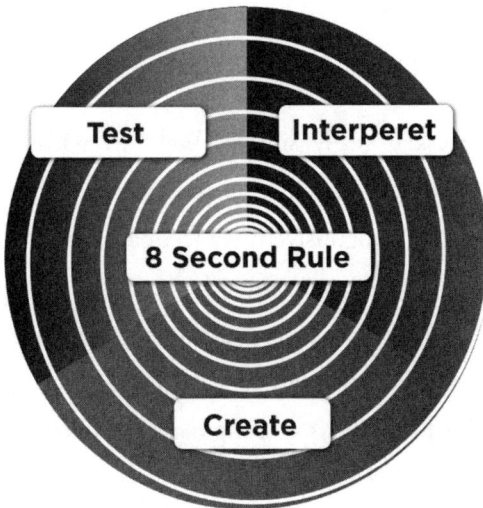

It cannot be stressed enough: When seeking markets beyond the demand horizon, instead of asking what potential customers want, you must show them your proposed solution to determine whether they want it or not. This cycle repeats until you nail the eight-second rule. Each time you test, you get closer to hitting the mark.

The Rigor Process

The rigor process was created to put actionable, substantive stages into the iterative prototyping cycle and facilitate the drive to eight-second success. It helps solve the riddle of how to build what people can't articulate. It's focused on unearthing real user needs from within potential demand.

The process is really simple. We start with a broad concept. That broad idea is something that meets a general need. Progressively, via feedback and through a series of questions, we refine the concept. From there, we immediately get into prototyping, which gives us something that people can actually see and interact with. This process has a strong bias for interaction with real products because that's where you get the revealed preferences. And that's where you get the spark.

To reiterate, we're seeking to nail the eight-second rule through this process. The diagram starts with a concept and moves from that concept to prototyping, testing, and interpretation in a circular motion as we zero in on a highly resonant product. It's not good enough to A/B test or validate a hypothesis. Within the rigor model, we are zeroing in on the most tangible validation of user demand: recognition of the usefulness of a product and desire to obtain it.

With the rigor process, we are far more explicit about our expectations. We need to put the eight-second rule at the end of this or we won't know when we get there. To say that X is better than Y 15 times in a row doesn't necessarily lead us in the right direction. Rigor helps to refine the value proposition down to a point where it is possible to nail the eight-second rule, giving a purpose to this iterative prototyping.

There's a good dynamic at play here, which is that the best business models move in concert with user needs. When you find that spark, there often is a business model that naturally meets that spark and generates, if not a new business model, then the natural fit for an existing business model. Whether it's advertising or lead generation or sales of premium content, those things often fall in naturally when you find exactly how a user wants to use your products.

Shouldn't I Just Go Lean?

The lean start-up approach has done wonders for creating awareness that new products must be validated and tested.[14] That has led to a significant improvement in the ability of companies—start-ups and established companies alike—to make better product and business decisions. Hypothesis testing has added a needed level of form and precision to product development. But, in its popularized form, lean doesn't provide precise insight into the creation of products for unmet needs. Specifically, the lean method was born in, and is suitable for, testing options that are in the realm of the *known*, those things that have already passed into the visible range on the horizon.

Why? The lean framework was derived from Japanese lean manufacturing, where every scientific test had the ultimate goal of doing one or all of the following: increasing efficiency, increasing quality or cutting costs. Those are operating goals, ripe for tactics that refine solutions within a known set of constraints. They are

---

14 Ries, E., 2011, *The Lean Startup,* New York: Crown Business

easy to measure and easy to establish when sequential tests move you closer to or farther from your ultimate goal.

Innovation doesn't work that way since it deals with the *unknown*. We are looking to find the very faint signal of potential demand beyond the visible horizon, and that requires a different, precise approach. To do that you need to use a framework that is created to seek out the signal of user demand and explore it. It is not looking for a simple measure of "this is better than that" but a real understanding of the emerging need. At its simplest, this is about putting a very specific type of hypothesis in place, the eight-second hypothesis, for direct exploration.

Increasing Success in Accelerators

In the past few years the concept of business accelera-tion has gained immense favor. By providing entrepre-neurs with a working location, mentorship, potential leads on funding and an opportunity to soak themselves in the energy of their peers, investors seek to increase the return on their investment and influence the odds of success. The movement started out within early-stage technology circles and has expanded to universities as well as reaching into every professional and vocational pursuit. There are now accelerators for agriculture, nonprofits, health care, biotech, insurance, financial services—almost everything imaginable.

As many accelerators as there are, there is only one goal: to generate new businesses. Yes, there is a focus on the creation of new technologies. Yes, there is a belief that by founding companies, we are creating jobs and solving important social conundrums. But at its simplest, the atomic level of value creation, accelerators are seeking to generate economic returns for those involved by starting viable businesses. And I suspect that when they are being completely honest, simple profitabil-ity isn't good enough. There is the hope—maybe even expectation—that within the batches of accelerated businesses, there is that one company that will make the history books and be a multibillion-dollar success. The stakes are high.

By definition this means that accelerators are working with exploration of potential demand. What's puzzling is that the majority of the activities of accelerators are suitable for known markets and known businesses within the range of current demand, not the unknowns of potential demand.

To put it a different way, most of the resources provided by accelerators are peripheral to the systematic and repeatable discovery and validation of new businesses. They are missing the mark and not impacting the activities that are most important for increasing the likelihood of success for their companies.

Let me explain. Extraordinary returns are achieved when a company creates a uniquely useful solution for a need that isn't currently met and is held by many people. As we know from our understanding of the demand horizon, these needs are never expressed clearly by the potential market. We also now know that a humble process of demand exploration through interviews, search analysis, big data and competitor analysis can make discovery and validation of markets a far more certain pursuit.

So the primary purpose of an accelerator, and the most important function for an accelerator to provide, is to assist its companies in the focused and systematic exploration of user demand. This is the area of expertise uniquely required by new companies. Office space is helpful because it gives teams a place to sit. Capital is useful, but only after a market has been validated. Mentorship is a wildcard, and can lead to as much confusion as it does benefit for the entrepreneurs when mentors provide conflicting theoretical advice.

By focusing on the exploration of potential demand, and truly understanding the nature of emerging markets, an accelerator can impact the success of its companies in a way that increases outsized returns and repeatable success.

Five actions accelerators can take to improve results:

1. Create a culture that de-emphasizes entrepreneurial ego and vision, replacing it with an
   attitude of curiosity and exploration;

2. Offer expertise and even facilitation of user conversations to explore market needs for participat-
   ing companies;

3. Provide access to tools that facilitate demand
   discovery, such as search engine data, competitive market data and behavior analysis;

4. Coach a company on interpreting and acting
   on various stages of demand identification as it
   relates to that company;

5. Select mentors who are prepared to guide
   companies through the product/market fit
   odyssey, providing their experience within that
   framework. Big names matter later, not now.

By creating companies with validated markets
and real data that substantiates the achievement of
alignment, investors will find more value in those
companies and have a far better understanding of how
application of their capital can help the company grow.

CHAPTER SIX

The Sweet Spot of Continuous Innovation

*"Fresh activity is the only means
of overcoming adversity."*

— JOHANN WOLFGANG VON GOETHE

Perhaps you've started a new business that's been running a little while or maybe you've got a business that you'd like to rejuvenate. Either way, for this phase, we are focusing on the innovation situation for a business that is functioning, has an existing market and is seeking to remain relevant to its customers. In this situation the innovation task is essentially the same, with the difference that there is increased risk in disrupting the existing business and there is a benefit of richer data to observe behavior.

The question now is how to keep a business fresh? How to keep it alive? How to avoid the seemingly inevitable cycle that leads to decline? Sometimes that cycle is short; sometimes it's long. However, if you're not careful about how you manage an existing product or an existing set of products, decline is inevitable.

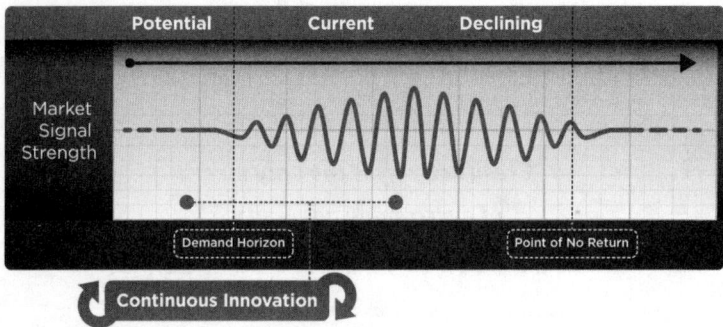

The sweet spot is about finding a combination of new exploration and existing operations.[15] It's about balancing the tension between market risk (unknown) and operation risk (known).[16] This is the classic inno-

15 March, J. G., 1991, "Exploration and Exploitation in Organizational Learning," in *Organizational Learning: Papers in Honor of (and by) James G. March*, 71–87

16 Crossan, M. M. and I. Berdrow, 2003, "Organizational Learning and Strategic Renewal," *Strategic Management Journal* 24, no. 11: 1087–1105

vator's dilemma[17]: once you find and build a business, there are a whole host of new expectations and responsibilities about operating that business. When the revenue flows, it becomes hard, often nearly impossible, to continue to take risks with the core business. This is especially true if investors expect steady, unfaltering growth. It may seem to make significantly more sense to operate the existing business and minimize change. However, long term sustainability requires that there be continuous "truing up" between the product and ever-evolving market need. The sweet spot is about finding this balance. It's the balance between unknown and known, change and stability, and market risk and execution risk. Market risk is how well a company can find new ideas, often from within the realm of potential demand. Execution risk is how well a company delivers within a known market, or current demand.

The perfect example is the computing industry. I was at Compaq just after the consumer PC had sprung up. There was a time when all computers were just computers, regardless of the usage purpose. But eventually a need developed. The consumer market wanted more gadgets and more buzzy stuff such as cameras,

---

17 Christensen, C., 1997, *The Innovator's Dilemma,* Boston: Harvard Business Press

high-end speakers and rows of extra buttons. The enterprise and commercial markets were asking for more consistent, reliable, swappable parts for easy maintenance.

When the consumer market sprung up, all of a sudden computers began to seem really slow. The industry started to focus on processor speed, RAM capacity, and other technical advancements. In the period when the consumer desktop personal computer industry was growing fastest, feature selection was driven predominantly by technical advancements. The computer business was all about faster speeds and forever-advancing specs. That was the heyday of the PentiumX and Pentium(X+Zillion). Consumers didn't even know why they needed all of the advertised features, but a higher number in processor speed, RAM and disk size was deemed to be good. This led to built-in obsolescence of products and very predictable sales growth for manufacturers.

That couldn't last forever, however. Eventually we didn't need new computers. They had gotten so fast that we didn't need to buy new ones as frequently. At some point computers became fast enough for almost everything anybody ever did. You could do word processing without waiting; you could browse the web without waiting; and you could run an Excel spreadsheet or an accounting package on even a low-priced computer. These "feeds and speeds" measures as they were called, just didn't matter any more. That industry, specifically Compaq, Dell, and Gateway, focused on the progression of Moore's law. It was (and is) common to have spreadsheets that define future capabilities in terms of the speed of the processor and the hard disk density, and consequently, the ability to project new configurations. Computer manufacturers marketed solely on the promise that the computer was big and fast.

Amid the perceived certainty of spreadsheet-driven product planning, those companies completely lost sight of the fact that people don't love computers; they love the capabilities that computers provided in their lives. Users want to be connected, to be more informed. They want the ability to be more productive. That's why there's been such a massive shift in corporations within the computer industry. The "speeds and feeds" approach that so many of these companies still cling to has completely lost its relevance. That's an illustration of the danger of falling out of the sweet spot—specifically, becoming so focused on the operational side of the business and current demand that maintaining relevance and alignment with user need is lost. The sweet spot, then, is staying in touch with consumer needs and continuing to adapt proactively as demand evolves.

The sobering fact is this: if your business is operating in a known market, with current demand, it's likely to decline unless you stay on top of evolving potential demand and introduce new products or refresh existing ones. How do you recognize when it's time to start thinking about innovating new ideas and new products?

First of all, "If you never stop innovating, you never have a dilemma." What that means is that a balanced company will always innovate with a portion of its resources and stay in tune with the market as it evolves. Then, as the company grows that market, it can continue to serve its customers. In fact, many companies enjoy the ability to influence the way demand materializes because they have earned the trust of their customers—think Amazon. That's the essence of market leadership.

A company that does this really well—a balanced company—will be the one that keeps innovating. At the very beginning, when a company is starting up, the market risk is often 100 percent. So 100 percent of the company's effort is put into innovation. This is the situation when you are trying to figure out what's new or significant in an unknown, or potential market.

Then, as you find that business and demand moves into the current phase, deployment of resources shifts over to roughly 80 percent to support operations and revenue activities. That means keeping 20 percent of resources focused on continued exploration of potential demand.

The key is to not let resource allocation slide all the way from 100 percent innovation to 100 percent execution. That happens too frequently. You need to find a way to slide up the percentage dedicated to innovation.

Regardless of whether you have balanced execution and innovation from the beginning, or you have lost your way and need to reestablish active connection to your customers and users, there's a pretty basic set of tools to use. What's needed is renewed effort in demand discovery.

The core idea is that companies need to stay very close to the specific ways their customers are expressing their needs. For instance, in the computing business, it's fantastic that all of a sudden we now have more powerful computers on our desks and more powerful computers to carry around. Yes, having a lightweight form factor was important, but the real need driving demand for light computers was overlooked. People wanted computing devices to integrate naturally into their lives. When you're carrying around a computer the size of an encyclopedia, it doesn't naturally integrate into your life. About five years ago the astute observer would have noticed that traditional computing via a miniature desktop computer, shrunk down to book size, wasn't enough to ensure the future of digital life. Tablets and smart phones were created to meet the true demand of users. Small laptops, in the form of netbooks, were created as the next step in the evolution of a size and weight reduction as represented in a manufacturing planning spreadsheet. This was a significant miss in terms of meeting user demand.

How could that gap between current products and unmet potential demand have been discovered more confidently, or by more than a handful of companies, especially when people couldn't imagine a tablet? Traditional market research doesn't necessarily give us the ability to extract from people what they don't know they want. The tools behind the demand horizon do. They work because we look for *expressed* needs, not what people *say* they want.

In some ways the activity of staying fresh within the realm of current demand is identical to the demand discovery principles within potential demand. The same discovery techniques of search engine query study, usage observation and exploratory user conversations apply here. Those are the tools in the tool bag of demand exploration.

The differentiating nuance is that, with a business that is currently operating, more signals for gaining insight are at your disposal.

Four Techniques for Discovering Demand

Search: As explained earlier, search engines are extremely useful for uncovering user demand. When people look for a new way to solve a problem, more often than not they go to a search engine. They put in their own terms to see if there's an answer out there. With an existing business and a current customer base, for items related to the products and services you offer, try making a search engine available to your customers as a site search or industry search capability. Publicly available information can be helpful for making product creation and revision decisions, but even more useful is the query stream generated by your own customers as they search your site or app to solve problems.

Usage data: Observe and explore the usage pattern of your products. Within publicly available web analytics packages, such as Google Analytics, KissMetrics and Chartbeat, lie very powerful tools for understanding what users are doing, where they are spending valuable time and from where on the site they are leaving. The same is available from a mobile app data provider such as Flurry. These analytic capabilities can be powerful for product creators and business leaders when viewed with the specific goal of learning the forms and patterns of user demand. In addition to providing intelligence on web usage in connection with existing offerings, these tools are extremely useful for observing web usage relevant to new product ideas.

User conversations: Take your existing products out to new/competitors' users for a conversation. This will provide a fresh and objective view on the perception of your offering. As before, don't ask, "How are we doing?" or "How do you like this?" People automatically move into the hypothetical and your exploration conversation turns useless. Ask interview subjects, "What do you think this does?" Again, in addition to careful conversations about mockups and prototypes, the best thing you can do to try to understand user demand is to look for what users already do and the ways in which they are trying to solve their problems.

Competition: Look at the market presence of other players in your space. There are tools for finding the search terms that drive traffic to those sites. For instance, you can look at the terms that lead to a click from the search engine to a competitor's site. This will give you a very clear idea of what is in users' minds as they seek out the competition.

What Keeps a Company in the Sweet Spot?

What are some of the hallmarks of a company that's good at rolling in the sweet spot compared to one that's heading for decline? The difference shows up in the balance of innovation and operations.[18] The balance is extremely difficult to establish and even harder to maintain, but a healthy company puts a certain portion of its efforts into running and optimizing existing businesses while also creating a safe environment for the exploration of new and revised products. Both activities must operate concurrently. If there's too much innova-

---

18 March, J. G., 1991, "Exploration and Exploitation in Organizational Learning," *Organizational Learning: Papers in Honor of (and by) James G. March*, 71–87

tion and exploration, profits suffer. If there's too little, decline is inevitable.

Companies that don't have a demand-driven culture of innovation are easy to spot. I went to the Consumer Electronics Show this year and I looked for companies that were operating on old push-based market approaches and losing touch with customers. I found exactly what I was looking for with Sony and Toshiba.

Every year, consumer electronics companies come to CES to showcase the latest and greatest new technology. Two years ago, the big focus was on the 3-D television. It seemed as if every TV manufacturer was convinced it had to make a 3-D television. They were really pushing this 3-D television idea, and it seemed completely odd to me. Every single big consumer electronics manufacturer displayed them and to get the full effect, you had to put on the special 3-D glasses. I walked away with a massive headache, not only from the glasses but also from trying to understand why anybody would want a 3-D television. I came to the conclusion that this whole 3-D TV thing was a bust.

So it was really interesting to go back last year to see if they were able to work out the problems of the 3-D television. It turns out that this year the 3-D TV was all but gone and the focus was on 4K televisions, which have the highest resolution, most beautiful picture screens that I've ever seen in my life. They're massive and they are superthin. And they are suffering from exactly the same problem as 3-D TVs. There is no market demand.

If that sounds familiar, it's because these companies are following the "feeds and speeds" path. It appears their products are driven by anything but the discovery of consumer demand. Is it because they're pursuing something transformational that's going to require people to buy more TVs? Yes. Is it because Moore's law is driving the progression for ever-more-powerful components? Yes. Is it because there will be a massive boom in sales if they can make other TVs obsolete? Definitely. Does the 4K TV exist because most TV buyers want one or will want one any time soon? Probably not. We're getting so far beyond the point where people are motivated to go from 1080p to 4K. Maybe eventually 4K will matter, but it's not a need that can be identified and quantified in the realm of potential demand today.

Samsung seemed to be a notable exception. Yes, the company is playing the 4K television game, but it is also putting huge effort into potential demand. It doesn't have a large presence on the computing side, but it is a very strong player because it is a big leader in the mobile phone and tablet space. That comes from its awareness of how even a massive company can stay on top of those trends and be a leader.

The majority of the big, traditional, consumer electronics players are focused on technical breakthroughs, but it's not a technical game anymore. Capabilities have progressed to the point where any company looking at winning customers through better technical specs is completely off-base.

My Experience with Innovation and Market Risk

Back in 2003 at AOL my team had the idea of starting a new destination search engine. It was an idea that came out of our user data. By looking at click and scroll patterns we saw that, very often, people searched for very specific things. There was a clear need for content such as movie times, maps and turkey dinner recipes. It was possible that we could build a search engine that delivered this content, not just links out to the web where it might exist. We could meet those needs in a unique way because, as a content publishing company, we had access to a lot of really interesting and valuable content. Our users were looking for richer results. They weren't just looking for lists of blue links. We saw the opportunity to create a search engine that delivered content in the form of news stories, movie reviews—anything relevant to the users' query. There was also a

Even great companies such as Amazon have to risk failure occasionally. Amazon failed with its search engine, A9. It decided to go after search when there was no clear signal in the market that there was room for a new search engine. That's proof that some of even the great companies experience failure when they go after a market without clear resonance.

solid business plan that showed we could create a meaningful business out of it. All we needed was to reinvest roughly $10 million of profits (less than 5 percent of the EBITDA of the core search revenues) back into the new business to launch and market it.

This opportunity was right in AOL's strike zone.

I pitched that idea upward to my executives and the response I got came from the typical, purely operational, quarterly-driven mindset: "Yes, we'll invest in this if you promise me that it can be profitable in the first fiscal year." My obvious response was, "No. I can't promise that." My executives at the time wanted the certainty of an operating business and all of the short-term pressures that implies when we were trying to create a long-term opportunity out of potential demand. It was a big idea and it was dismissed out of hand because execs had an operational mindset. Would it have worked out? Could AOL have established itself as the first content-driven search engine? It's hard to tell, but because of a lack of willingness, the opportunity was passed by without validation.

Is your organization built for innovation? A good way to know is if the culture and financial structure you have in place identifies and encourages people to create products that can push the edge and be factored back into the business. I believe companies that have such a structure can stay strong indefinitely, but such structures can be very difficult to keep in place year after year because of changes in employees as well as the performance of the company. It's a difficult thing to keep the right people in the right place. However, sustainable, leading companies find a way to do it.

Rolling in the sweet spot is about finding the right balance of innovation versus execution. You've got to get efficient. You've got to find that audience and that market that you can draw profits from. Sticking with only one market, however, leads to decline. Being able to balance efficiency with new exploration allows you to develop new products that can find their way into execution and begin to carry the momentum forward. Rolling in the sweet spot is about keeping the focus on underlying human needs.

Late in the demand cycle, things begin to look a little bit different. As we get into the next chapter, we'll talk about when to sunset, how to sunset, and how that feeds into recycling. Staying in that sweet spot can be done if you're willing to let go of your "feeds and speeds" mentality and if you're willing to invest and take those risks to continue to find the customer. It can only happen if you realize that it's critical—not just a luxury—to continue to innovate.

CHAPTER SEVEN

Managing Decline

"You and I do not see things as they are. We see things as we are."

— HENRY WARD BEECHER

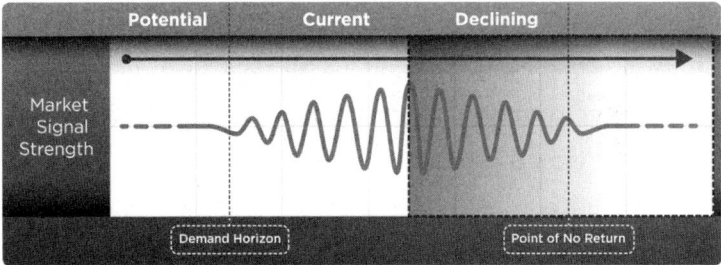

The operative question is how to identify a company or product that is heading into decline.

Human nature has a tendency to lead us to believe that things will continue on their current course indefinitely. That's true about humans in business as well. The default assumption is that to manage a business effectively, you should stay on the course that has worked previously. On the contrary, it is far more accurate to assume that a business is constantly moving away from its customer demand and risking decline.

A company, in the natural cycle of success, will progress from the discovery of user demand into the creation of a corporate machine to support that business. This machine will include sales, marketing, finance, accounting, and so on. Over time, however, that user need will move, seeking new or evolved solutions. It will change because of competition and because users become more sophisticated. Corporate structures, no matter whether in a large multinational or in a start-up, will create a path and inertia all their own, independent of the original demand. That strength and inertia makes it hard to balance continued truing up with user demand as it evolves. This is why the companies risk progression into decline by default.

In the previous chapter we covered the concept of the sweet spot, and how a balanced company maintains a productive relationship between market risk (unknown) and operations risk (known). But what if decline has set in to the point where deterioration of the market is obvious and inevitable? It's great to recognize that constant innovation is necessary to stay in touch with your customers and users, but how do you recognize when it's time to set an alternate course for the business? There are a few signs.

First of all, as a business matures and the gap grows between what customers want and the total number of available customers, customer acquisition costs go up. It could be that the product has penetrated the majority of its potential market and there isn't an obvious new market to replace it. It could be that your potential customers have moved to a competitor. Perhaps you're just losing relevance in some way or other. When customer acquisition costs begin to go up, that's usually a very early sign that the dynamics of the market have changed.

Customer acquisition costs are always going fluctuate, but staying on top of the cost trend is important. By the time the business machine is built, companies understand how to acquire customers. Finance and accounting track margins, but can creep up slowly, often within parameters that the machine is prepared to accept. Year over year, month over month, quarter over quarter incremental rises can add up without notice. Rising costs can be accommodated over time and not be recognized as a significant trend of increasing customer acquisition costs.

Consider the scenario when the product is in the sweet spot: customers are flocking to the solution for a real need and costs are relatively low; the market is actively seeking a solution. When the demand dissipates and the seeking behavior decreases, acquisition costs go up and warning bells should start ringing.

Another warning sign is when word of mouth declines. Through social media, companies are now capable of monitoring what people are saying about their product. If there is less and less buzz about your products and company, decline is a serious possibility. Because of social media, word of mouth is now easily trackable. Take the time to acquire and put in place tools that allow you to measure how word of mouth works for you over time. You don't have to buy the high-end social monitoring tools. A simple solution such as free social media monitoring tools (look for them on your favorite search engine) can keep you on top of a huge amount of social mentions. One of the leading indicators of a growing separation from your core customers is that they just give the product or company less mindshare. That might not show up in traditional market research, but it's certainly going to show up if you're tracking social mentions. And *mentions* are specifically what customers say, how they say it, and with what frequency.

There's one more warning sign that is really interesting, but it is also very hard to spot, initially. It's when your customers have become increasingly inflexible. What that means is that as you release new or updated products, they are less and less likely to be adopted. Your customers have become rigid.

That means that the people who are experimenting and actively trying new things—the ones who are vital for growth—are going somewhere else. You're left with the customers who, to borrow a phrase from *Crossing the Chasm*, are laggards. Those users are sticking around because it's more of a problem to change, so they continue to use a substandard product despite there being a better alternative out in the market.

That inflexibility can show up in a range of different ways, whether it is an unwillingness to try new products as they are introduced or constant griping about changes in the interface or the brand. All those things should be seen as an indicator that you now have a more laggard-type of user base.

The whole concept of decline is that the company that once met the user demand loses touch with that demand and loses touch with its users. Users only have a certain set of core human needs and those needs never disappear; they just change. Change occurs as our tastes mature in accordance with new technologies and we become oriented to how these new things work. A company that understands a human need and is able to adapt and meet that need through multiple product cycles or multiple product permutations truly understands and stays in touch with the customer.

> The whole concept of decline is that the company that once met the user demand loses touch with that demand and loses touch with its users.

CHAPTER EIGHT

Reduce, Reuse, Recycle

"If it's inevitable, act as though it's immediate "

— UNKNOWN

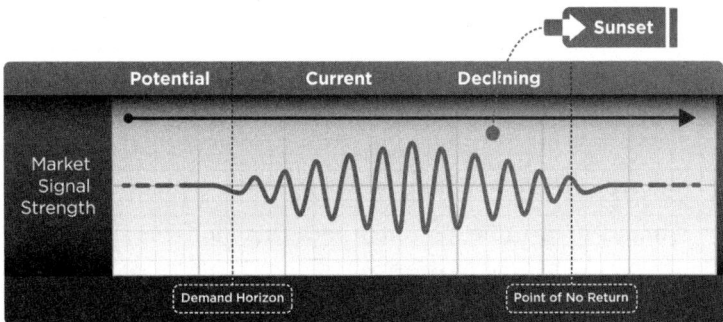

Sometimes demand is gone. Demand for a product or similar products can definitely decline to a point of no return. We've discussed the telltale signs for businesses looking to spot trouble on the horizon. We've also identified the actions that can get a declining business back into the growth territory. But the question remains: are you stuck in a death spiral? There certainly comes a point when a brand or product expression loses the ability to be cost-effectively reinvented. In fact, it's possible that some things can never be reinvented. There is such a thing as a point of no return.

It's important to recognize when a product has declined to the point where it should be dealt with as a cash cow—or dying profit machine. The answer is very basic. At some point products will decline to where they're not profitable, and no reasonable investment can revitalize them. If there aren't enough buyers to cover the costs of producing and marketing a product, it's not profitable to do so anymore. The point of no return is simply the point where costs will be larger than revenues. That seems really obvious, but here's where things break down. People have a fondness for what a product or a brand used to be, so oftentimes they don't necessarily recognize that it is in decline or remain unrealistically optimistic that recovery is possible.[19]

---

19 Szulanski, G., 1996, "Exploring Internal Stickiness: Impediments to the Transfer of Best Practice within the Firm," *Strategic Management Journal* 17, special issue: Knowledge and the Firm: 27–43.

This is the time to be ruthless and honest, Instead of investing in a brand in decline, costs are reduced and profits are maximized until there is no more cost to reduce and profits are zero. This can often be predicted with a high degree of accuracy. The math must be done with a sharp focus in order to understand when costs are projected to outstrip profits.

When you know that number, you can then decide whether your customer base is worth reinventing or allowing to decline down to that point of no return. Unfortunately, most humans don't work that way. Even the most responsible manager has a thing called agency risk. The manager's job is to manage. Most managers and executives are not going to raise their hand and say, "I've got a dead one here. By the way, my job is attached to it and I don't know what I'm going to do next." Those who serve as agents for their company are motivated to be optimistic about their product's success, or, at the very least, they are motivated to be quiet about its decline. They continue to ask for incremental investments and they continue to tell a story that doesn't necessarily reflect the cold reality.

There is massive waste in the corporate world, caused by unrealistic views of when the revenue line will decline past the cost line. Operations would be much more efficient if objective decisions were made to minimize costs so that a business or product could be wound down and the audience, which we know is rigid, introduced to something new.

The two big mistakes occur when decision makers don't recognize decline or cover it up. Either way, the result is that they don't necessarily minimize costs and continue to invest in their business even though, essentially, no amount of invested money could turn that business around.

Most often, it's not that companies invest in large amounts and with concerted effort to reinvent a business. It's that investment is applied incrementally. The harm in not recognizing the terminal nature of the situation is that it delays people's ability to take broader steps to recycle their audience at the end of a product's lifetime.

By the time a business begins to decline, often the people who created it and had understanding of the original demand have long moved on. The managers who now operate the business don't necessarily understand the alignment between demand and solution that it took to create the business, or how the original leaders got in touch with users' demand in the first place.[20] When the current leaders see the process of decline beginning, it's very common for them to move on to other projects as well. So a declining business or product can be left with an inexperienced or improperly motivated leadership team. That has a huge impact on both accelerating decline and the implementation of improper/incremental action.

This highlights the fact that there's a skill in selecting the right people to get the most out of a business on its way down. You're not likely to have the people who brought it to success; they've probably moved on already. So what are the hallmarks of the right person to put in charge of optimizing your decline?

Each stage of the business cycle is operated by a corresponding personality best suited to it. For example, the people who are good at looking for and understanding market risk tend to be risk takers. A company operating in current markets will often be staffed with people who do a very good job of hitting quarterly numbers and understanding exactly what it takes to satisfy customers. They're working on an operational delivery model.

---

20 Szulanski, G., 1996, "Exploring Internal Stickiness: Impediments to the Transfer of Best Practice within the Firm," *Strategic Management Journal 17, special issue: Knowledge and the Firm:* 27–43.

Recycling: The Alternative to Shutdown

Unfortunately, if your business has dipped deeply into decline, dramatic action is needed.

We've spent a lot of time to the left of "Current" (demand) and "Potential" (demand), which is where the horizon sits. We've also covered the cases in which a business should be shut down, before the point of no return.

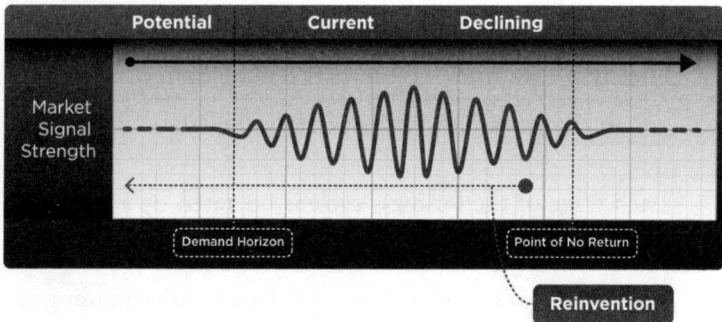

Recycling occurs just before the point of no return. You know you're at the point of no return—first and foremost—when your profits are gone. Another indicator is that your audience size has decreased to the point where it's just a shadow of what it once was and there's less (perhaps about 10 percent or less) demand for your product.

You end up in a situation in which you're not making money, you're serving an old audience, and/or usage is declining toward zero. If the audience is not profitable and it's shrinking, recycling can be a powerful tool because it allows you to tap back into what originally created the brand.

At this stage, people may even believe in the brand, but it just doesn't match up with what they need at this point. The goal is to recapture, in a transformation of the product, the untapped value that was originally met by that product. Remember, core user needs of communication, transaction, information discovery, and so on, never change; they are just transformed by new technologies and market taste. So there is often still hope. It's just a matter of taking that risk and being bold enough to reinvent and realign with that need.

Why does it need to be dramatic? Once you're approaching the point of no return, incremental innovation is too little and too late. Significant effort is required to reverse the momentum. We're not talking about 20 percent of your resources on innovation and 80 percent to keep the ship running.

We're talking about risking cutting off major portions of your user base. Remember, these users and customers may be very rigid in their willingness to adapt to new products. This means taking a hard look at the essence of your brand or product and going back to tap into that legacy to either gain a new energy with the market's existing users or attach to a new audience. The idea is to keep the positive legacy but shed what is thought to be irrelevant by the market. Ideally, you create a break in the customer's mind and attach to new attributes or to a new audience.

When there's no prospect for reinvention or the appetite's just not there for reinvention, and when the user base is rigid and revenues are declining to where it's clear the business will be unprofitable, it's just obvious to close it down. It's absolutely black and white. At this point it's about business and when it becomes unprofitable to operate a line of business or when it falls below an accepted low-water mark, it's time.

It's no different than what Steve Jobs did with computing. When Apple had a single-digit share of the market and was pretty much only selling to universities, Jobs came back and kept the brand name but essentially created a completely new company. From desktops and printers to iPods, iPads, iTunes and laptops. Reinvention is possible.

CHAPTER NINE

Beyond the Horizon

"And those who were seen dancing were thought to be insane by those who could not hear the music."

—FRIEDRICH NIETZSCHE

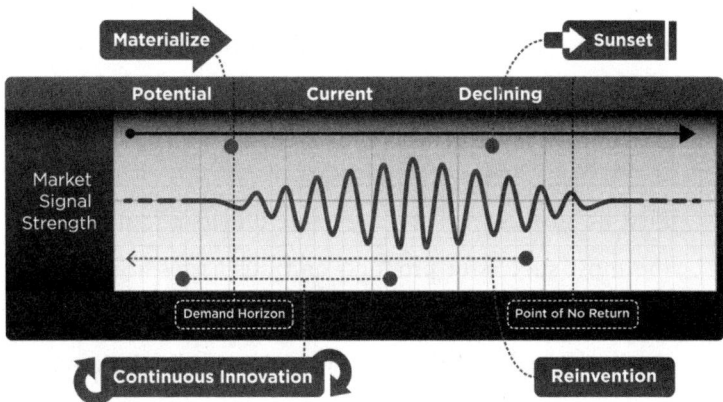

Today, someone somewhere is walking down an office hallway with a prototype that has the potential to set the course of the next 10 years. It may be within a big company, complete with executives, managers, sales teams, marketers and a big finance group. It's just as likely it's a few people in a makeshift office/garage, with few resources beyond their creativity and drive. Regardless of the setting, there are revolutionary products being created today that have the potential to impact our lives in the most fundamental ways.

But which ones will succeed? Which products will find resonance in the market? Which entrepreneurs and intrapreneurs will achieve their full impact? Which companies and divisions will become the next multibillion dollar successes? The answers to these questions have historically been too hard to predict. However, we now have a very solid idea of the attitudes held, the exploration conducted and the activities performed by the product creators who will succeed.

First of all there will be a humble understanding that the most successful products and businesses arise out of relentless pursuit of user demand. And that demand sits in the realm of the unknown. Above vision, above passion, even above experience, investigation into what users want, yet can't express, is the key to beginning the product/market alignment process.

Second of all, that understanding will be explored and refined through observation, objective study and carefully conducted conversations. User needs will be unearthed methodically and iteratively, with the sole goal of understanding what the needs of the market are and what solutions may deliver the best fit for users. Success will be hard to achieve and yet easy to identify. The opportunity will begin to assume its true form, and its fit with the market will be understood as potential customers can readily identify what purpose the solution serves and seek to obtain it for their own use.

Third, that company will have a working understanding of the demand lifecycle, how market demand transforms from a faint signal into a very clear expression of need as it crosses the demand horizon. When the market materializes, they'll know to bring the right talent to build out the operational capabilities of the company and shift to execution mode. There will also be an understanding that, as the product grows, a portion of their efforts must remain focused on tracking and adapting to user needs as they evolve. There will be a balance between exploration of potential demand and operation within current demand, always in tension, but always balanced in direct orientation to market needs.

As much as that sounds like the perfect, hypothetical, demand-centered company, this is also the path that many of today's transformers and tastemakers follow intuitively. Companies such as Apple, Google, Amazon, Facebook, and Twitter all use a form of this approach. There are numerous examples of companies that have been able to stay relevant and vibrant over long periods. This book gets at the root of this most troubling business problem and provides a user-driven model for understanding what's happening. With demand horizon you can address the challenge—whether it's the thorny problem of bringing new products to market, fighting decline in a business that's been strong historically but lately has been facing a competitive threat, or figuring out when to shut down a business.

The demand horizon model is comprehensive. It allows all business leaders and product creators to reinvent old-school, push-style thinking and elevate their strategies and actions onto a completely new plane. Once you understand this model, you can readjust any business to be in alignment with user demand. That's true for companies of all sizes and businesses at all stages of growth. Perhaps the most powerful thing about the demand horizon model is that it's prescriptive; it helps you approach the entire range of innovation possibilities. It's an approach that balances the discovery of new opportunity with the necessity of operations

The promise of this mental model is that it provides the conceptual tools to reorient any business at any stage to a simple, new level of potential or effectiveness. If you're looking for a way to validate a new start-up idea, understanding demand and isolating it with rigor and the eight-second rule will provide great insight. Whether your business is growing or declining, whether it's suffering from competitive risk and struggling to stay relevant over time, there's a way to take this model, assess where your business fits with it and figure out what the next steps might be in order to stay fresh.

Users are in control and we have tools at our disposal to understand what they want. By climbing up to the crow's nest of big data and exploratory user conversations, we can use our telescope of interpretation and data analysis to see beyond the currently visible horizon of current demand.